NIETZSCHE
IN ITALY

GUY DE POURTALÈS (1881–1941) was born in Berlin to an aristocratic family who later settled in Switzerland. After attending universities in Germany, Pourtalès moved to Paris in 1905 to study literature at the Sorbonne. He published his first novel in 1910, married in 1911 and, claiming Huguenot ancestry, acquired French citizenship in 1912. During the First World War he served as a translator for the British army in Flanders. Victim of a gas attack at Poperinghe in 1915, he was later diagnosed with pulmonary tuberculosis. Pourtalès soon departed Paris for the slower pace of the Château d'Etoy on lac Léman, where between 1926–1932 he applied himself to romantic biographies of musicians. Pourtalès was prolific as an essayist, reviewer and polemicist, whilst maintaining a vast correspondence with other European writers including Stefan Zweig. In 1937 his autobiographical novel *La Pêche miraculeuse* finally won him a major literary prize, but the loss of his only son during the battle for France in May 1940 sent Pourtalès into a steeper decline. He died in Lausanne in June 1941.

WILL STONE is a poet, essayist and literary translator of French, Franco-Belgian and German literature. Will's previous translations from French include *Rilke in Paris*, by Maurice Betz (Hesperus, 2011 / Pushkin, 2019), *Emile Verhaeren: Poems* (Arc, 2013), and *Georges Rodenbach: Poems* (Arc, 2017). Those from German include *Messages from a Lost World: Europe on the Brink by Stefan Zweig* (Pushkin, 2016), *Friedrich Hölderlin's Life, Poetry and Madness* by Wilhelm Waiblinger (Hesperus, 2018), *Surrender to Night: Collected Poems* by Georg Trakl (Pushkin, 2019), *Poems to Night* by Rainer Maria Rilke (Pushkin, 2020) and *Encounters and Destinies: A Farewell to Europe* by Stefan Zweig (Pushkin, 2020). Will has published four critically appraised collections of poetry, the first of which, *Glaciation* (Salt, 2007 / Shearsman, 2016), won a major international prize. He has contributed essays and reviews to the *London Magazine*, the *TLS* and other publications while his poems have most recently appeared in *Poetry Review* and the *Spectator*.

NIETZSCHE
in
ITALY

Guy de Pourtalès

Edited, translated and with
an introduction by Will Stone

PUSHKIN PRESS

Pushkin Press
65–69 Shelton Street
London WC2H 9HE

Nietzsche in Italy was first published as *Nietzsche en Italie* by Bernard Grasset in Paris, 1929

First published by Pushkin Press in 2022

9 8 7 6 5 4 3 2 1

ISBN 13: 978-1-78227-728-6

Designed and typeset by Tetragon, London
Printed and bound by Clays Ltd, Elcograf S.p.A.

www.pushkinpress.com

Contents

Introduction

Pourtalès was forty-eight years old when he wrote *Nietzsche in Italy*. Midway between his musical biographies, the Nietzsche book, essentially a protracted essay evenly sliced into brief chapters, sits slightly askew from them, seeming a little like the black sheep, the less visible maverick in the well-oiled sequence of audience-guaranteed works on composers to either side. Perhaps this is why it failed to be picked up by English language translators at the time, unlike the venerable Liszt and Chopin tomes. Yet in contrast to the more long legged "romantic" biographies, the smaller *Nietzsche in Italy* sparkles with a timeless quality some ninety years on, and despite its age, often feels light footed and impressionistic, suggestive and enquiring rather than over assured, its seams stretched with conviction. Scepticism and deliberation over academic authoritarianism. Pourtalès, the descendent "Good European", is both in awe of this titanic spirit and feels genuine sympathy for the necessary suffering of the body that bears it; thus the reader travels on under the sign of a noble humanism. Pourtalès seeks to paint an image of an exceptional mind stretched to its limits trapped within a living being steadily transformed into a position of historical uniqueness by that being's own strength of will and always against the odds. For Pourtalès, Nietzsche is both liberated and constricted by a self-imposed mission that becomes more messianic as he finds himself alone in unexplored terrain and there accrues revelatory insight. Reality and its wearisome imp of the perverse is his daily curse and a body which frustratingly won't give him enough hours of relative health to distil that intellectual firewater from the mind. We witness with unease and increasing sympathy Nietzsche's restless journeying, the mental load borne from the attempt to radically adjust the restricted sight of an age. We are made painfully aware of this exceptionally lucid individual's precarious existence in an inwardly degenerating society, advancing scientifically and materialistically, but retarded psychologically and spiritually by clinging to handed down Christianity and "foreground conclusions". The drums of nationalism grow ever louder as the philosopher leans ever closer to the page. Nietzsche is a European traveller and seeker by philosophic heritage, self-determination, cultural wont, peripatetic inclinations and climate induced exile, while Pourtalès shadows his master in all these, the robustness of his pan-Europeanism underpinned by his ease of movement between German, French, English and Swiss language and culture. Author and subject share a common heritage, a perceived future which is irrevocably European, where borders define neighbouring cultures eager to converse and reciprocate. The confinement characterized by militarism and nationalism are anathema to them. Neither man is prepared to pace the drab corridors of monolingualism. Movement in a free space is everything.

Pourtalès ensures we follow the relentless combatant at a discrete distance, though we still have him in plain sight, as he is gradually acted on by the restorative climate and atmosphere of the South, antipode to the Northern darkness of Germany (a trope set in motion by Goethe and his *Journey to Italy*). We witness Nietzsche at successive stages of his development as the myopic visitor follows his travelling trunk onto the platforms of his preferred Italian cities. Naturally Pourtalès includes the major dislocating events and their aftermath; the unsavoury break with Lou Salomé after the marriage snub, the disenchantment and severance with Wagner, the unexpected sanctuary of a quiet quarter of Venice and Bizet's *Carmen*, on to the downfall in Turin so wilfully dramatized in the public imagination. Yet one senses whether in Genoa or Messina, in Rapallo or Venice, in Sorrento or Turin, we are rather awkwardly waiting in the wings to see how long this lonely 'professor' can survive with his dwindling reserves of air as the expected literary response fails to come. For Pourtalès then, Nietzsche's Italy is a series of chronologically linked stations of necessary regeneration and subsequent creative breakthroughs. This idea has of course been taken on by a number of authors and Nietzsche scholars since then, and details have been necessarily fleshed out, but Pourtalès was surely the first to bring these Italian ports of call together, to construct the map of topographic salvation in a way which shows the recurring holistic attributes such locations offered Nietzsche, who let us not forget habitually returned to those places which had served him well in the past, hoping for similar deliverance, or because distracted by thought or some symptom of his sickness he clambered onto the wrong train.

Yet even the casual observer can see that Pourtalès' account is a little idiosyncratic, selective rather than comprehensive, and focuses more heavily on Nietzsche's experiences in Venice,

Genoa and Sorrento, whilst Lake Orta for example gets barely a mention. Although he mentions Nietzsche, Paul Rée, Lou Salomé and her mother travelling there before Lucerne and thence Tribschen in the spring of 1882, there is no mention of the time spent in Orta, most significantly the fabled kiss between Nietzsche and Salomé on the terrace of the romantic Sacre Monte above the lake, perhaps suggesting something more than intellectual admiration on her part and which Salomé, mercurial to the end, later did little to deny or confirm. "Whether I kissed Nietzsche on the Sacre Monte I do not know now". The stricken Nietzsche looked back to the Orta days with Salomé as the zenith of their relationship, when a definitive union seemed possible between two increasingly interweaving souls walking together, batting thoughts back and forth, within the romantic ambiance of the medieval lakeside town, on the tiny island of St Giulio with its mysterious convent squeezed in atop a rock, in the pine woods around the Sacre Monte studded with ancient frescoed chapels. Later, as he painfully watched Salomé pull away, Nietzsche defensively attributed characteristics of spite and cunning to the woman who rejected his hand, gruffly declaring 'the Lou of Orta was a different being'. Why Pourtalès omitted this legendary moment in the Nietzsche Salomé story nevertheless remains unexplained. Perhaps he felt its resonant ambiguity an unnecessary distraction.

This piece would not be complete without mentioning one of Pourtalès' key correspondents, whose shadow hovers over this essay because of his own text on Nietzsche published four years earlier in 1925. Stefan Zweig's essay "Nietzsche", the third part of *The Struggle with the Daemon: Hölderlin, Kleist and Nietzsche* could well have informed or inspired *Nietzsche in*

Italy. Did Pourtalès read Zweig's work? Potentially, probably, presumably... the two were working in similar fields, both were engaged in monographs and biographies, they respected each other and corresponded. But does it really matter, for though they are both devotional tributes to a heroic intellectual struggle, they are quite different books. Zweig's "Nietzsche" excels in its compelling portrayal of Nietzsche's physical sickness and apartness, his lonely, pauperized existence restlessly moving between down at heel pensions in the Alps and coastal resorts and back to his writerly base, the rented first floor room in the Durisch house at Sils Maria, plagued by no reply from the world below the Engadine plateau. In contrast the primary focus for Pourtalès is the author's biographical leitmotif; music, as crucial presence and life force, as inspirational backdrop and inward filament running through Nietzsche's mental universe, intermittently glowing and powering up the faltering generator. The soon to be realized Wagner book was simmering away in Pourtalès' mind when he wrote *Nietzsche in Italy*, but it is here he makes the first inroads, performs the groundwork and gathers the required momentum. After reading Pourtalès' little book one can certainly understand better not only the way the releasing power of music served to reinvigorate, even recalibrate Nietzsche's mind, but how a particular arrangement of notes literally held him back from the abyss, from the destruction he fully expected, most importantly just long enough to carve out those dark-veined yet shimmering last works, those stars formed from a point of origin which no longer exists but whose long-travelled light we see so vividly now.

WILL STONE

EXMOOR, MAY 2022

Cast of Characters

FRIEDRICH NIETZSCHE (1844–1900)

German philosopher, philologist, classical scholar, poet, composer and cultural critic who attempted to reveal the false values that underlie Western societies clinging to outmoded religious concepts and to provide a new existential framework for an idealized thinking man of the future, the free spirit.

LOU ANDREAS SALOMÉ (1861–1937)

Russian-born intellectual, poet and essayist, later psychoanalyst, who had relationships with some of the most influential artistic figures of the late nineteenth and early twentieth centuries. These included Nietzsche, whose marriage proposal she turned down, and later the poet Rainer Maria Rilke, whom she accompanied on lengthy trips to Russia and continued to support and counsel until his death in 1926.

PAUL RÉE (1849–1901)

German author, physician and philosopher who met Nietzsche in the summer of 1873. Rée, then a doctor of law and five years younger than Nietzsche, had already written a dissertation in Latin on Aristotle's *Ethics*. They shared a mutual interest in the French moralists and Rée's thought later influenced Nietzsche during his middle period from *Human, All Too Human* (1878). Whatever level of friendship existed between Nietzsche and Rée following the former's ill-starred marriage proposal to Salomé, it could not survive the aftermath.

MALWIDA VON MEYSENBUG (1816–1903)

German writer best known for her *Memories of an Idealist*, the first volume of which was published anonymously in 1869, as well as her friendships with intellectual figures such as Nietzsche and Wagner. She invited Rée and Nietzsche to the Villa Rubinacci in Sorrento in the autumn of 1876, a moment of transformation for Nietzsche and the genesis of his later philosophy. Von Meysenbug was the first woman to be nominated for the Nobel Prize in Literature, in 1901.

RICHARD WAGNER (1813–83)

German composer, conductor and theatre director known primarily for his operas, who towers over nineteenth-century music and culture. Wagner is famous as an innovator, whose groundbreaking methodology changed the course of musical history. His most ambitious project was the monumental fifteen-hour *Ring* cycle. Something of a controversial figure today, Wagner's legacy, however impressive, has been tarnished by his antisemitism.

COSIMA WAGNER (1837–1930)

Wife of the composer Richard Wagner and illegitimate daughter of the Hungarian pianist and composer Franz Liszt. She married the aristocratic German musician Hans von Bülow in 1857 but divorced him in 1870, having spent a year living with Wagner at Tribschen. Later that year she married Wagner and bore him three children: Isolde, Eva and Siegfried. After Richard's death in 1883 she dedicated the rest of her life to maintaining the Wagner cult. Her diaries (1869–83) provide a trove of detail on the composer's life and thought.

PETER GAST (1854–1918)

Johann Heinrich Köselitz, German author and composer, was given the pseudonym of Peter Gast by Nietzsche. Their friendship developed during Nietzsche's time in Basel and Gast would read to the half-blind professor and take dictation. Köselitz was a key figure in the preparation of Nietzsche's works and devoted himself to furthering Nietzsche's exposure. For his part, Nietzsche, in a bid to throw off Wagner's Northern trappings and embrace the Southern style, somewhat overestimated Köselitz's talent as a musician. From 1899 to 1909 Köselitz was conscripted into Elisabeth Förster-Nietzsche's "Nietzsche-Archiv" in Weimar. Always suspicious of the motives of the chief "curator", he left in 1909, tainted by collusion, after he assisted in the publishing of the highly selective edition of *The Will to Power*.

ELISABETH FÖRSTER-NIETZSCHE (1846–1935)

Formerly close to Nietzsche and two years his junior, Elisabeth Förster-Nietzsche was his sister. Elisabeth and Friedrich became more distanced following her marriage to Bernhard Förster, a publicly visible German nationalist and antisemite, in 1885. To her brother's horror, they established a racially sanctioned German colony, "Nueva Germania" in Paraguay, in 1887. After her tormented husband's suicide in 1889, she continued to run the colony with an iron fist. Returning to Germany directionless in 1893, she had a lucky break. Finding her brother now an invalid whose writings were catching fire across Europe, she swiftly adopted the role of safeguarding his legacy and thus was able to edit his writings in ways which furthered her own nefarious political and racial convictions.

NIETZSCHE
IN ITALY

"The most beautiful lives are, to my mind, those that follow the communal and human model, with order, but without miracle and without extravagance."

MONTAIGNE, *ESSAYS* BOOK III, CH. 13

"Who today then is still a Christian in the sense that Christ wished us to be? Myself alone perhaps, though you are quite prepared to think of me as a pagan."

GOETHE, CONVERSATION
WITH CHANCELLOR VON MÜLLER

"I believe that superior men and therefore the saints, the true saints who are superior men, are at the same time the beings most capable of love. Yes, the development of any great discovery, of any great thought is always accompanied by the most extraordinary emotionality. At the root of intellectual life there is emotionality. It would be impossible if the highest intelligence did not ally itself with the finer elevated qualities of the soul."

JULES SOURY, INTERVIEW REPORTED
IN HIS NOTEBOOKS BY MAURICE BARRÈS

To Paul Valéry

Permit me, my dear Valéry, to offer you this modest and imperfect essay on a man whose abiding grandeur you have properly felt and whose vertiginous heights you have elucidated. Perhaps it would not have occurred to me to place your name at the head of these pages, if the coincidence of a recent encounter had not led us to speak of Genoa. It is a city you, like Nietzsche, have loved, and where, like him, you found yourself in your twentieth year in anguished spiritual combat after which you resisted plucking your glory at too young an age, when, on the contrary, Nietzsche decided to waste no time in seizing his own. You were right to wait and he was not wrong to hasten. Barely ten years after his first Genoese winter came that darkening December of Turin.

And then, did you not write of him: "I could not conceive that this violent and vast mind had not finished with the unverifiable…" Nor, my dear Valèry, have we finished. For as soon as, in the works of the spirit, love or hatred comes to take its part in creation, the unverifiable extends and claims the central point of our reasonings. However, if it is to be at the expense of their solidity, perhaps it is not without adding something to their movement, to their partiality: that they become vulnerable, but at the same time alive.

It was from this impassioned aspect that I sought my Nietzsche. Possibly I merely yielded to those "bad workable feelings" that you recommended by way of approach. Then you must excuse me: the following sequence of images can only illustrate, with this Prince of Thought, the absurd but tenacious logic of the heart.

JULY 1929
G. DE P.

I

A Traveller Without Baggage

Any being who observes a love they have lived with for a long time fading inside them calls to death for assistance. But death rarely responds to such a summons. So one must live, sadly; must survive. The wounded man raises himself, bandages his wound as best he can and takes flight. "Travel," they urge him. So he departs with his shadow. Perhaps you will encounter him months or years later, healed. Apparently healed. But deep down, no one ever recovers from a withered love. He is not the same being that you once met. Yet it is him, his eyes, his smile, his hand. But he is enveloped in that "resounding solitude" of which Saint Jean de la Croix speaks, where his mute realities have taken on a quite different voice.

When in the autumn of 1876 Nietzsche set foot for the first time on Italian soil, he was fleeing his past, he tore his youth from his heart. This thirty-two-year-old man, brimming with still-intact spiritual power, had just made the first great sacrifice of his happiness. He renounced the secret love, the deep love which for more than six years had disturbed his life with a kind of hopeless intellectual dream, for Cosima Wagner. He was renouncing her illustrious husband, "the master" as all referred to him, the man of Bayreuth, whose apotheosis he had just witnessed in a theatre erected to his pride and who now appeared to Nietzsche—following this fall into popular glory—like some form of imposter, a simple showman of genius. He cleansed his soul from a protracted sickness in which he had indulged for years, a disease he had taken for strength, pure strength, but where he now discovered nothing more than coarse tufts and putrid vegetation. The young professor from the University of Basel left for a spell of convalescence to Genoa and Sorrento. For some time now, his sight had been seriously impaired. He suffered excruciating migraines. This slight intellectual, who shelters his gaze behind thick glasses and hides a gentle smile beneath an enormous moustache, first stops at the thermal baths of Bex, in the canton of Vaud, then, one mid-October evening in Geneva, boards the train for Italy.

One can imagine what such a journey would have been like in the narrow little oblong box that the carriages were then on our old P-L-M.[1] The young professor sits there quietly, reservedly, between two German ladies, who like him are also travelling to Genoa. Conversation begins and will last through the night with the younger of the pair, Mlle Isabelle von der Pahlen, who will remain for ever "entranced". It is true that Nietzsche is a conversationalist the measure of which Germany has rarely seen. He is in high spirits. He knows everything. He effuses with profusion and he more than anyone knows when to become silent and seed that silence with ideas. In his pocket he carries a copy of La Rochefoucauld's *Maxims*. At which page did he open it? I open my copy and come across this: "Everyone speaks well of his own heart, but no one dares speak well of his own mind."

Quite so, but why? Because our heart has been given to us, so we are not responsible for it. It's all about being happy. While with our mind, which we have formed, a certain modesty is required. While it is exciting to have multiple souls, as Barrès claims, it is impossible to have multiple hearts. Multiple by soul, we are one by the heart. The soul refines and divides itself, but the heart always remains whole and untamed. The soul makes the personality, but the heart makes the man.

Nietzsche feels he has much heart and little soul. Later he will say the opposite. But for the moment he thinks less of his work than of life. To live, what can that signify to this professor threatened with blindness, pauperized, unknown, precociously enfeebled, and yet who senses that he carries within him the intellectual gospel of tomorrow? To live can only mean to contemplate, to work, to write. To write, that is to say to explain oneself, to express oneself, to load the other pan of the scales—that of dream—with all that fate has not placed in the pan of reality and thus force a rebalancing of the beam. In short: to compensate for the inadequacy of fate. He smiles silently with his myopic gaze, for the compensation will be tragic: the manuscripts he has crammed into his briefcase are dynamite capable of exploding the earth. They arrive in Genoa under a splendid sun and Nietzsche drops right away on to the bed, his head is shattered, his eyes still steeped in night. In the hotel room, shutters closed against the sun, he recovers himself over the next twenty-four hours. Now his escape is already compromised by the walls of a new prison: sickness. His headaches and pains have tortured him to such an extent over recent months that he resolved to ask the Basel authorities for a full year of leave. It would surely be better not to live at all than endure this martyrdom. Total rest, a mild climate, walks, dark rooms, this is what he asks of Italy. Would she, too, refuse them to him?

He reflects. What has he accomplished so far? A demanding career as a student and then as Professor of Philology, interrupted by the war, a few years of teaching during which he recognized that linguistics is the cornerstone of all philosophy and, as Proudhon said, the natural history of human thought. He met Wagner, and his simple symbols were transposed into complex music. And for a long time he lived, he, the Greek philosopher who wanted to be Latin, in society with the pretentious phantoms of the Germanic forest. He published his *The Birth of Tragedy*,[2] a major work. Nietzsche smiles: a beautiful book which thrust him into the front rank of his generation. A dangerous, ridiculing book (he smiles some more) which contains the buds of those good restorative poisons intended for Christian and Romantic humanity. He then published some of his *Untimely Meditations*,[3] then his *Richard Wagner in Bayreuth*,[4] the ink of which is barely dry. All of this—excepting the first book—remains unknown to the public. Whatever. Wagner himself hardly suspects that this young apprentice has prepared the quinine meant to bring down the fever that he engenders in men. Nietzsche was still in Bayreuth only a few weeks ago, but only to carry out the severance. He's healed now from the sting of the old serpent. He will now heal thousands of others. The South, Latinity, this is the prescription that he writes out for himself. Did he not dare to pen these words to the triumphant master just a few days ago, who had also left for Naples: "May Italy remain for you the land of beginnings." Beginning what, exactly? At the age of sixty-three? No, it is Nietzsche who will begin. Germany has been an overlong school textbook for him.

It is now all about unlearning, in order to take back, to free oneself, to make oneself free.

Man is no longer above all else a religious animal or one of knowledge, as has been solemnly believed for centuries, but simply a living animal. What replaces in his poor head that old fear of death is his modern fear of not living enough. Our time is that of a passage from an outdated moral state into a new moral one. Hence our anxiety, our evident unrest. The task of the artists will be to provide men with new themes of formation as powerful as those of the past. This is why it is not futile to review in the light of a psychology which is loving, comprehensive, perhaps even enthusiastic the enigmatic figures or violent souls who came before us. Let us be like the poets of the "silent seers".

And let us be sick, if we have to. Because there is a morality of the healthy and a morality of the sick. The sick, he will one day say, have no cause to be pessimistic. However, it is often the healthy who reflect on death the most and live in abject terror of it. But that makes sense. Nietzsche, who was during his fifteen great creative years a dying man, searched for the meaning of life. The grace granted the artist is the power to make his suffering objective, to release it by channelling it into a form. The sick Nietzsche did this by seeking the meaning of life, as against Tolstoy, who sought the meaning of death.

One evening, Nietzsche reappears in the hotel lounge and offers to lead the ladies through the streets of a Genoa that he has never seen. But he has attended the lessons given by the historian and critic Jakob Burckhardt in Basel. He knows how to explain the architecture of the great palaces to cheerful businesspeople and marvels at the thought of what made them so spacious, so solid and so beautiful. Was it not, for this all-conquering aristocracy, the superlative expression of its taste for life? These houses proclaim a sense of the immortal. To build is to affirm that we live through strength. The Genoese lived and wanted to survive. Building is the conquest of mind over matter, and perhaps it is best to see how, in Nietzsche's words, matter does not exist.

He is charmed by the glittering boutiques, the jewellery stores on via degli Orefici, he delights in the crowd, contented to touch these humble mercantile truths. He buys a brooch for his sister. Then he takes leave of the two baronesses with that refined politeness which affords him a tender air, and a few days later, after a crossing by sea, he disembarks in Sorrento.

II

Port-Royal of Sorrento

In Sorrento, Nietzsche is the guest of an elderly German lady, a devotee of Wagner's, internationalist, socialist, utopian, one of those good, intelligent and idealistic persons such as one observed in the era of corsets and the first novels of Pierre Loti, in those cities which they preferred to call "cities of art and poetry". Malwida von Meysenbug had a sense of comfort and a genius for friendship. She had just rented the Villa Rubinacci in which to spend the winter, receive friends and live a while in the neighbourhood of Wagner, newly instated at the Hotel Victoria, five minutes' walk from her villa.

This Villa Rubinacci is a simple and bright house, paved and flanked by a pair of terraces, one of which overlooks the gulf, the island of Ischia, Naples and Vesuvius; the other looks on to dry stone walls, lemon groves and the mountain close by. Malwida von Meysenbug occupies the upstairs rooms while the gentlemen have the run of the ground floor. The first solitaries of this little German *Port-Royal*,[1] organized by an old maid in a suburb of Naples, are three in number: Friedrich Nietzsche, the young student Albert Brenner, and Paul Rée, a doctor of Jewish letters, a subtle philosopher, for some time already a friend to and admirer of Nietzsche whose manuscripts he deciphers and copies with evident competence.

They live in a contemplative and learned atmosphere, each contented with their own company. The windows give on to the umbrella pines, the sea. The morning is devoted to work and meditation. Nietzsche wakes at six o'clock and sets to work immediately. At noon the midday meal is taken together. In the afternoon they sometimes bathe, go for walks together or alone, according to the mood of each (often for three hours). In the evening, after dinner, there are readings, usually entrusted to Rée.

This first contact of Nietzsche's with the South is a profound joy, an immense hope. He lacked sufficient strength for the North, those countries where souls are artificial and slow-paced, hungry for rules, all belted and braced with prudence. But there is no question he will have enough spirit left for the South. It seems now he can breathe fully and easefully, rediscover that intellectual good humour which is the ideal state for creation. And despite his physical infirmities, the migraines, the vomiting that confine him to his room for days on end, he labours on, ever conscious of an inner strength. All the more conscious, no doubt, that a mere hundred paces from his room "the other" is also at work, the master, the foe. Yes, that old Wagner whom he loves and hates, that old monster from the other race of men, the race of victors, of buccaneers. Invincibly attracted, the two adversary friends lie in wait for each other. On occasion they will take a stroll together, filled with reciprocal pride, concentrated, combative and bristling with contrary electricity.

Wagner has sensed all that his former disciple now reproaches him for, the weakening of his thought, the questionable quality of his successes, the sensuality of his fallen art. And the young Jansenist questions him with a cold glance, with a word dry and deep, unsettling the lapsed atheist of Tribschen, who has recently transformed himself into a knight of Christ. What is your faith worth, old man? Where are your spiritual weapons, renegade?

One evening, shortly before the composer's departure for Germany, Nietzsche and Wagner take a walk together, side by side. After so many others over the course of the last seven or eight years, this is to be the last, the one from which they will never return. Certainly, neither is under any illusions on that point, since as they set out on this beautiful late-autumn day they remain silent, burdened with memories, like those lovers who have reached the furthest point of their passion and who know without saying it to themselves that it is impossible for them to advance. They follow the gulf, then ascend through the pine forest to some viewing point. And there, gazing over the sea into the far distance, Wagner finally declares in a low voice: "A landscape ideally suited to a farewell." Then, as if the inevitable hour of this confession had come, he speaks of *Parsifal*. But not as a work of art, rather as an authentic religious experience. It is no longer a question of music, but of repentance, of penance; no longer about an art of life, but about the grace of a good death and an absolution obtained by the supreme work in atonement for one's sins.

The sun sinks and disappears on the horizon as the celebrated one explains himself at length before the unknown, wearer of the discomfiting look of keen intelligence. What might he be hiding under this sudden flood of words? His fear of the Last Judgement? His reconciliation with the Church, with the pious powers ruling the new Germany? And why not the simple fact that this about-face might incline the public authorities to finally lend support to the musical and poetic edifice which he has decided at the eleventh hour to crown with the cross? Nietzsche is unable to provide an answer.

And the other: "Come, my friend, have you nothing to tell me?" Nothing, indeed. Remain silent. Then Nietzsche writes in his notebook: "I am not in a position to recognize a greatness which is not sincere towards itself. To play a comedy with oneself arouses in me a feeling of disgust…" But is Wagner at this moment truly a comedian? No, surely not. He is in thrall to a feeling common to certain natures: suddenly, he is overwhelmed by the sense of sin. The pain leaves a sharp bitterness on his tongue. And *Parsifal*, this act of faith, will absolve him.

Nietzsche, motionless and internally quivering, this time smiles haughtily over the corpse of his most impassioned friendship. No remorse pricks his heart. Barely any regret for what he voluntarily relinquishes. One has to live for the new truths to combat the wretched cult of suffering, the pleasures of nothingness, the fraudulent values to which Wagner has committed his talent and strength.

Will they find it too hard, this crystal that no fault against the spirit or against love has ever tarnished?

Wagner and Nietzsche would not meet again. Perhaps Nietzsche never loved Wagner as much as at the moment they separated. He wrote later: "At the time of the final farewell, when we part from each other because feeling and judgement no longer go hand in hand, then we become closest. We come up against the wall nature has erected between us and the being that we abandon."

The three solitaries of the Villa Rubinacci continue their work, their readings, their excursions. They take with them in succession Chamfort, Diderot, Stendhal, Michelet, Thucydides and the New Testament. The Gospel of Saint Matthew moves them deeply. "The New Testament has rarely given so much joy to atheists," young Brenner wrote to his parents. But these are aesthetic pleasures. Malwida goes to look for a photograph of *The Last Supper* by Da Vinci, and of Jesus, Nietzsche opines that he was "the highest of human souls". If he rejects his doctrine and distrusts a morality where weakness is exalted, he is invincibly drawn to the man himself. This disarming and serious face pursues him. Now one of Nietzsche's old projects, the founding of a small secular convent for intellectuals in need of solitude, is often debated. Mlle de Meysenbug has just published her *Memories of an Idealist*,[2] and the gentlemen are decidedly won over by this socialist of Forty-Eight,[3] daughter of a minister, who knew the friends of Goethe and Humboldt and always remained, in the words of Daniel Halévy, "faithful to the true genius of women". Though not possessed of a superior intellect, she was an upstanding and courageous person, genial in all respects. They loved her. They also had a lot of fun shocking her. They collapsed many of her socialist ideas. And yet Nietzsche tactfully refrained from reading his manuscripts to her. In some men of the outstanding type, intelligence may blush. And precisely because it is of the higher type. They are in some way ashamed to possess such strength.

It was only following the departure of Rée and Brenner, when they were walking amidst the soft nuptial spring, that

Nietzsche presented his old hostess with a few leaves of the manuscript he was working on and which bore the strange title *Human, All Too Human: A Book for Free Spirits*.[4]"With what gentleness," she wrote, "with what benevolence Nietzsche was then animated!... How admirably his amiable and good nature balanced his destructive intelligence." Destructive, she said, expressing from the outset the objection so many others would make against the work of one of the greatest architects of liberated joyfulness that mankind has ever produced. For she, too, had read some of those rules of life which Nietzsche liked to scatter about his notebooks:

"You must neither love nor hate people."

"You must not enter politics."

"You must not be rich or needy."

"You must avoid the path of those who are illustrious and powerful."

"You must take a wife outside of your people."

"You must leave it to your friends to raise your children."

"You must not accept any ceremonies of the Church."

Refrain from publishing this quite yet, wait. Reflect... urges the old lady.

But Nietzsche smiles, because already, like all those who write, he envisions his book striding forth along the ways of the world, seeking out readers, enflaming existences, sowing fear or pleasure. He sees it acting, provoking thought and action, connecting him to the lives of other beings, participating in what will happen thanks to him and thus become movement. Now, of all the thoughts noted under the wide pine-parasol of the Villa Rubinacci, this one ought to be particularly coveted: true immortality is movement, "What was once set in motion is locked into the chain of all being, like an insect caught in amber, imprisoned and become eternal."

The book was "dedicated to the memory of Voltaire, in commemoration of the anniversary of his death". A commemoration also of the first great Nietzschean crisis of intellectual liberation. "Every sentence," he said later, "expresses a victory." Victories over romanticism, over emotive attitudes, over "idealism", Nietzsche's bête noire. Every error is calmly examined, placed in ice, not so much repudiated as frozen. When the book was printed, the author sent a copy to Bayreuth. En route it crossed with *Parsifal*'s libretto, which bore this dedication: "To his dear friend Friedrich Nietzsche, with his most cordial best wishes. Richard Wagner, ecclesiastical counsellor." Nietzsche was taken aback. Such provocation! Here were the clanging swords of Hunding and Siegmund in the clouds of Valhalla. Here was the duel with Wotan and the distant presage of the death of false gods.

III

Venetian Music

Nietzsche did not see Italy again until three years had passed, in March 1880. But now it is another traveller who travels, accompanied by other shadows, a more prodigious invalid, a more settled mind, purer, harder. These three years have whitened his temples (at thirty-six), hunched his body, loosed his fortune a little more from earthly ambitions. (I prefer to use this word "fortune" for one who really has nothing.) He gave up teaching for good. Pensioned off by the University of Basel, he is free and forsaken, he has traversed interminable physical sufferings, he has reflected much, worked hard, and he can write to Mlle de Meysenbug, "I have suffered so much, I have renounced so many things that there is no ascetic in any time you care to name with whom I do not have the right to compare my life in this past year. However, I have been richly rewarded. My soul has gained in purity and sweetness, and I no longer have need of religion or art for that. You may notice that I am quite proud of this fact; it was only when in a state of utter abandon that I was finally able to discover my intimate sources of consolation."

It is understood that Venice is the city of love. For Wagner it had seen the birth of *Tristan*,[1] the painful fruit of his break with Mathilde Wesendonck. For Nietzsche it was the blessed place of his convalescence. Not at all a "city of art", a "city of beauty", as for so many others a beautiful exercise in literature painted over with sunsets, a gleaming symphony of dead waters in which are reflected Casanovian dalliances. For the Nietzsche who escaped his pedagogical prison, Venice is nothing but the charming city of silence and liberated reflection: "the city of a hundred deep solitudes".[2] For him, no churches, no Tiepolo, Tintoretto, doges, Bridge of Sighs, no little Stendhalian eroticisms, no thieves, no carnival in eighteenth-century costume. The artist quivers only at the pleasures of thought cast in the music of words. (And it should be noted that he is by no means averse to pleasures or girls.) He never enters a museum, those repositories of dead dreams and exhausted ambitions. He has only a zest for life. He devotes himself to the happiness of men with whom he comes into contact but does not really see, seeking to furnish them with the spiritual justification for their impulses. He wants to make them freer, more aware, more joyful. To make them more men and less slaves. He wants to deliver them from their idols and restore them to themselves, rid them of false morals and social prejudices. "Immoralists", he called his kind, with harsh pride. How he has been reproached for that single word, the chaste, the teetotaller, too pauperized to afford alcohol or women!

Nietzsche takes up residence in the old Berlendis Palace on the Fondamenta Nuove,[3] constructed in the Baroque style, where he lives in a great room. Lined with marble. It's a twenty-minute stroll from Piazza San Marco, along silent alleyways, without dust, without sun. The shade of Venice, a marvellous blessing for his eyes and his head. Delights so endless that the book he is working on (*Dawn*) has long borne this working title: *Ombra di Venezia*. His life is meticulously organized. Work from seven or eight o'clock, a walk, a frugal meal. At a quarter past two one of his all-too-rare friends drops by, the one who urged him to come to Venice and has been loyal to him all his life: Peter Gast. His real name was Köselitz, son of a Prussian landowner, but a musician, a bohemian, who left home in his youth for Basel, where he became Nietzsche's pupil and dedicated himself to composing, for which he received no acclaim. For a long time, Nietzsche was his sole admirer. All those who love Nietzsche and know something of him will know this Peter Gast. He is the Pylades to this Orestes,[4] who respects Nietzsche and who is respected in his turn.

"How many tears have I given to your misfortunes?"

And how much time he has given to his work, this Gast, scribbling away to his friend's dictation, clarifying his notes, recopying his manuscripts, tending his fragile health, ever tactful and discreet, careful never to offend Nietzsche's brooding character, never to place a burden on this neuralgic intellect. "If my life is to have any meaning," he wrote one day, "it will be the active interest I took in that of Nietzsche." And indeed, that is how it was.

So, at a quarter past two, Peter Gast arrives. One and a quarter hours of dictation, conversation, readings. And then work resumes until around half past seven, when Gast returns and they have dinner together. More often just a boiled egg and a glass of water. On other occasions they go to Gast's residence, take turns at the piano, Nietzsche improvising, playing his own compositions in his somewhat dry and learned manner; a tireless Gast returns to the keyboard to recite pieces by the only poet who can rid them both of Wagner and restore them to the works of the old masters, to the purest of musical traditions: Chopin.

In Sorrento, Nietzsche listened much to Beethoven and often went in the morning to a wood of cypresses and wild roses which filled him with the harmonies of the allegretto from the Symphony in A major. In Venice he loved only Chopin. Of course, there exists a kinship of the soul between Chopin and Nietzsche. In these two invalids, these two passionate, chaste men, in these two loners, everywhere in exile, the dramatic exuberance of the life force resonates in union. Might I add here: a mutual pleasure in creating out of doubt. Perhaps you could also claim the pleasure of suffering with a noble bearing and, being conscious of this, to prefer some brief periods of crisis to all the sober simplicity of a carefully exploited glory.

Gast wanted to write a book on Chopin. Liszt had made one, and, let's be honest, it was a bad one. (Anyway, most of it is from the grandiloquent pen of the old Princess Wittgenstein.)[5] Gast felt there was plenty more to say, and he made two hundred pages of notes. Doubtless, Nietzsche assisted him with these drafts, and it is to be regretted that they remained unpublished, for what infinite subtleties must Nietzsche have had to say about a genius so close to his own sense of the tragic, a taste for aphorisms and for the collected? But, as we said before, often the most beautiful ideas, when they touch certain "sublime" beings, tend to lose themselves in the unreal.

It was in Venice, Goethe wrote in his *Journey to Italy*,[6] "that the meaning of the song was first revealed to me". So especially impressionable via the ear as he was, it is clear that Venice was also a most singular musical revelation for Nietzsche. City of a hundred profound solitudes; city of a hundred musical notes of the soul. That *Tristan*, poem of the world's forgetting, was hatched in Venice, like the "forgetting" of Byron's *Manfred*,[7] Nietzsche can grasp better than anyone. There is a perfume of oblivion, of death, of decomposition in this city of artifice whose very foundations are mouldering under the lapping of the heavy waters. Here the heart is as if diluted, and what lovers may draw from it is a mute warning of fading, the sigh of centuries, an eternal reminder of human solitude.

Tristan occupies an exceptional place in the Wagnerian oeuvre and, in some ways, positions itself outside his habitual inspiration. The Venetian influence has loaded these desperate pages with an accent of the intimate not evident to the same degree in his legendary dramas. This is what he later called "setting the admirable Venice to music".

In *Dawn*, Nietzsche also set *his* Venice to music, his interior Venice. Amongst the notes he makes on his walks or at café halts something resembling a new song can everywhere be heard. What was not yet properly fixed in his prose now unfolds in profound harmonies that underscore thought, and extend it into new regions to which classical syntax no longer has access. "That music has no need of words," he says, "is its greatest advantage over poetic art, which appeals to concepts, and therefore clashes with philosophy and science; but we don't notice a thing when music steals us away from them, leads us, seduces us." We might say that it is music that on occasion makes Nietzsche appear to lose his footing in his writings. But if it then becomes unintelligible, it is precisely because the melody opens other doors for us through which our gaze darts towards unsuspected horizons. Let us read in *Ecce Homo*:[8] "One more word for select ears on what I demand from music. May it be joyful and deep like an October afternoon. May it be distinctive, exuberant, tender. May its cunning and grace make it a sweet little woman... I shall never admit that a German can know what music is. Those we term German musicians, and above all the greatest, are foreigners: Slavs, Croats, Italians, Dutch or even Jews; and those that are German are of the stronger race, the one which has today died out, such as Heinrich Schütz, Bach and Handel. I myself still feel Polish enough to discount all music in favour of Chopin. I here except the *Siegfried Idyll*[9] by Wagner for three reasons (one of which without a shadow of a doubt is named Cosima), perhaps, too, some things by Liszt, who surpasses all musicians who were raised on the far side of the Alps. On this side, I could not do without Rossini and even less *my* South in music, our Venetian maestro Peter Gast. And when I say this side of the Alps, I'm really saying Venice alone. I am unable to judge the difference between tears and music."

In truth, there is a certain charm in reflecting on these intangibles. Concert-hall musings, where the head of a beautiful woman, a bust inclined in some moving attitude, make us wonder with pleasure that "there are so many dawns that have not yet shed their light". A Hindu proverb. Nietzsche loved it. He included it as an epigraph in the first draft of the book, which launched his campaign against moral superstitions. And later he added again, in an autobiographical note, this comment: "The absolute clarity, the serene disposition, I would even say the exuberance of the spirit which this work reflects, accords with me not only as regards the deeper psychological weakness, but more with an excess of suffering."

Such was this mandolin-free Venice Nietzsche enjoyed. For sure, he hardly experienced a dazzling youth, this philosopher struggling to become a lay Christ, when he set out on his spiritual way of the cross. For love, future humanity. For disciples, a penniless, struggling musician. We are a long way from those celebrated old Venetians: the mischievous and truly over-sated Byron, the snobbish Chateaubriand, the poignant Mickiewicz, the pretty Musset with his barber's beard. And even their friend Barrès—black lock of hair upon a yellowed ivory brow—who exalted a whole generation of young "free men" while we wore out our first shorts on the benches of the kindergarten. All of this picturesque literary scene tended to lose its colour as we grew up. Today, those so earnestly eloquent shades have long faded; their overblown ambitions merely bring a smile to our lips and the modest Nietzsche, loath to be a practitioner of decorous entanglements, moves us so much more in his unique demeanour, his ironic clairvoyance. His Venice has nothing to do with a platform on to which one raises oneself to strike an attitude. It's not about hotel-living with him, where you can take a few days off from the page for a round of pleasure. For Nietzsche, Venice is a melody of the soul, the prelude to his most authentic works. He said later, in *Ecce Homo*: "When I look for a word to replace that of 'music', I only find the word 'Venice'."

We recall that Wagner, one sleepless night, while working on *Tristan*, went to lean on the balcony of the Giustiniani Palace:[10] "And as I gazed down at the old Roman city of lagoons which lay before me, shrouded in shadow, suddenly from the deep

silence a song rose up. It was the strong and hard call of a gondolier watching over his boat, to which the echoes of the canal
answered even to the furthest distance; and I recognized there
the primitive monotonous chanting into which in the time of
Tasso his renowned verses were adapted, and which is surely as
ancient as the canals of Venice and their people…"

A quarter-century on, the muses made Nietzsche the same
gift. They desired an equilibrium between the poet of the senses
and the poet of the mind. And Nietzsche, without knowing that
the "sorcerer" had surprised the ancient secret of the city, wrote
to Peter Gast: "Last night brought me again, while I paused on
the Rialto bridge, a music that left me in tears, an ancient adagio,
so incredibly ancient that there simply couldn't have been an
adagio before this one."

This is where the true artists reveal themselves: they hear
and see beyond the vast "lost time" of humanity what others
no longer hear or see, but just unwittingly hum as a tune, vague
and wordless. The adagio that Nietzsche caught on the air of
that Venetian night is the same that inspired Racine. The same
that draws lovers on to trains bound for Italy. And if ever one
day it should happen to flood our own heart, we are astounded,
like the philosopher before us, that there could ever have been
another before to rival this.

IV

Piccolo Santo Genovese

In the landmark work he devoted to Nietzsche,[1] Charles
Andler observes that the philosopher "has always made an
admirable choice when it comes to a dwelling place". Indeed,
for many, the setting in which they live is the key to accessing
their interior landscape. And this is not so much a question of
sensitivity and "artistry", but the overriding need for intelligence,
spiritual comfort, and the absolute necessity of exchange and
union between oneself and the world. For some, the intimate
setting, the living room, the room where they will create are
of the highest significance. For others, it will be a matter of the
sky, the climate, the atmosphere of a city or the pleasures of
the surrounding countryside. Nietzsche had a noticeable love
for stone, whether it was the rough state of rock, or cut and
aligned in solid architecture. Genoa had particularly seduced
him by its aspect recalling a great bourgeois lord redoubtably
bound to the nobility of matter. Genoa appeals to those who
have an appetite for *things*. Chopin loved it, this professional of
the spiritualized in concrete. Paul Valéry lived there for a time,
and he left us these notes of his impressions: "What a unique

42

and complete city. It has no Canaletto, nor a Guardi; Corot painted only a couple of minor canvases there. None has yet exploited this inexhaustible mine of etchings." And no doubt the sympathy inherent to these three reflections on Genoa stems from the clarity of its architecture, from the construction of its terraces. "So visible a city, and present in itself; eternally familiar with its sea, its rock, its slate, its brick, its marble; in perpetual labour against its mountain."[2]

Nietzsche returned there in the autumn of 1880 and chose an attic room above a small grass-covered street, La Salite delle Battistine. The salty air, the daily walks along the military boulevards or the ramparts of the fortified enclosure, the old port pungent with fishy odours, such are his aperitifs. He refers to himself as the Christopher Columbus of a new America, an interior America, uncharted territory. He walks five or six hours a day, rests awhile on a wall, stretches out in a meadow or by the beach, absorbed in reflection, making notes and suddenly producing an abundance of the most sublime prose. Abundant with rhythms, ideas; at once bristling and Dionysian, furious and ecstatic. He even dances alone on a patch of grass to the music of his thoughts. Then he makes his way back to his labourer's room, exhausted but happy to have fired his weapons against Plato and against God. And the people of the neighbourhood always saw him alone, a book in his hands and his briefcase hung from his shoulder, so wise, so gentle, so courteous to those slight folk, who nicknamed him *"il santo; il piccolo santo"*. A good little Teutonic saint, so very poor, who would doubtless attract divine blessings to the shopkeepers of the upper town. Sometimes, they made him the gift of a candle to light his room or for his devotions. With humble heart, Nietzsche gladly accepted these marks of affectionate respect. "No alcohol, no renown, no women, no newspapers, no honours," he records in his notebook, "only the maintenance of the highest spirit and, from time to time, that of the lower classes, for it is as necessary as the sight of powerful and healthy vegetation…"

Could we French, in our mid-thirties, and even beyond, being so free and in Italy of all places, rigidly follow such an ascetic existence, as a Benedictine, and remain artists, poets, breathe the flower and the fruit of things without getting our teeth into them? Not understand penury as indignation or irritation, but simply embrace it? Suffer horribly in our body and gain only a surer reason to proclaim the sublime art of remaining healthy? Worship the vast, silent sky, the silent twilight, and gather all the words of silence to be assured that "there are only individual truths"? Finally, refuse everything so as to divine everything with ever more delicacy? Hardly would we dare evoke some garrulous compatriot, a painter on his uppers, a literary tourist before the image of this mighty lord of the spirit, so correct, so honourable, and those ideas that would wound and pierce like clear realities. "All my truths are to me bleeding truths," he said. Perhaps you might think from his pronouncements that he had fallen for socialism? Far from it. In this Genoese period we find in Nietzsche's work not only the harshest indictment of democracy, but the most haughty aristocratic spirit. Of course, this is only a question of an acquired aristocracy of thought, not that conferred by birth or wealth. The new genealogy of feelings will rise slowly into his mind, from the probity of the heart to that of the mind, to culminate in the only passion permitted to the moderns: the passion for truth. *Passio nova*. But if a passion exists, is there not also fever and delirium? Shouldn't the truth itself vibrate with some notion of sensual warmth? Do we wish only in order to know, or to savour the joy that knowledge bestows? Nietzsche is already coming up against his ultimate problem, and, as M. Andler says, "he will no longer be of the belief that the intelligence is there to think in terms of reality, but rather to refine our instincts". This is where his *Dawn* will end, that thick herbarium of thoughts slung from his shoulder like a botanist's box of finds. Sometimes he pulls out an orange, an apple, a crust of bread, which will do for his lunch. He adds a new note to the others. He is buoyant, with the feeling of his fullness, of his combativeness. He writes: "To give, to restore, to share, to become poorer, to know how to be humble in order to be accessible to many without humiliating anyone. To feel the weight on one's shoulders of so many wrongdoings, to have crawled through the subterranean burrow of countless errors in order to reach a multitude of souls by secret ways. Always to live in a kind of love and no less in a kind of egotism and self-enjoyment. To be in possession of an empire and to live concealed in renunciation." How, at root, he is a Christian, this future anti-Christ! How his father the pastor, his mother, his austere education at the college of Pforta[3] and even his stoic and Wagnerian youth moulded his soul without his being aware. We believe we are free, we become de facto free, we wish to pass intellectual acts on to others, but then of a sudden our hearts cast us off and refuse to clear the most seemingly easy obstacle from the past.

The "little saint" of the Fontane Marose quarter is yet to complete the book which will be the beginning of his crusade against traditional morality. He prepared his kit for war, stockpiled ammunition, freed his life from material shackles. He rid himself of bad masters, sensual enthusiasms, and even a good part of his most noble friendships. He only forgot one thing: to kill his heart. "Stay true to the earth." But of course. And she will compensate you. She will prove to you that you are not pure spirit, for she, too, remains faithful to you.

At the close of that spring of 1881, with *Dawn* now in print, Nietzsche sets off for Recoaro, in the Italian Tyrol, where his friend Gast joins him. Something new is simmering inside him, which the nearby mountain ennobles. But it is no longer philosophy, nor those stunning aphorisms that he carefully pastes into his notebooks. It is a violent poem which seeks to gush forth, a deep impetus of his entire being, to liberate that source which flows just above ground. The lyricism of new wisdom roars through the resounding cellar rooms of this intoxicated soul. "How can one state in a single word what all the energies I have within me are converging towards?" he wrote to his sister. He himself did not yet know, but that word would bloom from his mouth like the rose of some unknown species. He thought it was *Dawn*; but it was Zarathustra. "You are about to see," he went on, "how the thing is done that will make your name, at present hardly ringing out, immortal."

V

Zarathustra—Lover of Carmen

This "thing" had not yet been born. But it was conceived, that is to say expected and desired, by instinct. It filled Nietzsche with vertiginous enthusiasm. He bore it in his body like a powerful fruit, nourished by his blood and his marrow. It was to be a terrible offspring, this one, a child who would overwhelm the world with the sound of his music. For it is under the sign of music that he will baptize in advance his son Zarathustra. And because "the phoenix of music flew around him", his "Hymn to Life" (arrangement for mixed choir and orchestra) was born at the same time. "It will be sung one day in memory of me," he would say, as they will sing the idea of the eternal return, this law of worlds and civilizations, this affirmation of life.[1]

Nietzsche flees to the high mountains of the Engadine, a refuge of even more exhilarating purity than Recoaro. Through a chance conversation with an unknown traveller on the road to St Moritz he discovers Sils Maria, its rocks, its larch tree, the Fecht valley. It is there that Nietzsche, in early August 1881, receives his vision of *Zarathustra*, his "heroic idyll". The rapture is such that he walks in these solitudes weeping tears of joy.

He sings, he indulges in crazy utterances, he feels eminently dangerous, "like a machine that could explode". And there is a payback for his interminable suffering, his perpetual headaches, his near-blindness, his moral and spiritual isolation, his impoverishment. Never again will he envy the happiness of men. He has "placed his hand on millenniums":

"One to whom work gives the highest sensation, let him work, the one to whom rest gives the highest sensation, let him rest; the one to whom order, imitation, obedience give the highest sensation, let him obey. But let him be conscious of what gives him the highest sensation, and not shrink from any means to achieve it. This is eternity."

"Not to look to distant hopes, unknown blessings, but to live in such a way that we wish to live again and live in eternity as we have lived. This life is your eternal life, for all is eternal return," Nietzsche notes this momentous moment. "On that day I was passing along the shore of the lake of Silvaplana, by way of the forest. Beside a pyramid-shaped boulder not far from Surlej, I halted. It was there the thought came to me... six thousand feet beyond man and time."

An illustrious passage in the history of ideas. The place touched by this great memory. But it was but a minute of pleasure in the arms of that most chaste woman: eternity. "I have never yet met a woman with whom I wanted to have children except this woman I love: for I love you, O eternity." Without doubt a mistress who will prove barren. Do you somehow have to be German, and a philosopher to boot, in order to relish such an abstract convulsion with this level of intensity?

It is necessary to return to Italy for a period of recovery following such a prodigious pleasure. In October, Nietzsche returns to Genoa, where he finds himself again with great pride and gaiety, quite the Prince Doria.[2] But he also re-encounters his physical suffering, his "dog", as he calls it, his faithful hound, indiscreet, impudent, comical, intelligent. It helps him think. It forces him to think. Good, helpful dog, worthy of its master, for a new book is drafted in three months and written in only one: *The Gay Science*.[3] But we must acknowledge there are respites from the barking and biting of the beast. Sunny spells of light-heartedness. During one of these, Nietzsche discovers Bizet's *Carmen*.

It is something of a surprise for us—just a little—Nietzsche's sudden enthusiasm for this Carmen with her rose and fan, her Don José and her bullfighting, her imperious Escamillo. But it is important to view this heady intoxication with Carmen as primarily a remedy for Wagner. Wagner, an old disease which still sometimes re-emerges, reigniting the fever for which it has been so difficult to find a cure. First, Wagner was pitted against Chopin. Music versus music. For all philosophy is a series of events of the soul and finds it symbol only in music. Chopin versus Wagner. Peter Gast versus Wagner. Brahms versus Wagner. And now, here is Bizet—a man by dint of his Latin heart wonderfully passionate and balanced, yet with a Gallic discipline, clear as the Mediterranean sky, leaning on old Iberian folklore—and also against Wagner. With what joy Nietzsche would have embraced this unknown young Frenchman, alas by then dead. He notes the date of his discovery (on 27th November 1881). He begins a letter to Gast with "Hurrah! The French have a huge musical lead over the Germans on this essential point: for them, passion is natural and healthy, not forced and unhealthy as with Wagner. Bizet, Mérimée,

Stendhal, Chamfort, Genoa, those things which accord and amplify one through the other."

Even the weather is in tune with his joyfulness around this Southern Christmas. An exceptional sweetness that slips gladly into the heart. A prelude to love, of which Bizet has just provided an energetic, innocent image and all loaded with pure cries of instinct. Not those convoluted loves of Siegmund or Wotan, but passion brutal and clear as a blade, on the borders of morality; the healthy taste of pleasure, the essential law of nature. "Gradation, contrasts and logic," he notes on the score of *Carmen*, which he sends to Gast. Nowhere does he see vulgarities, but, on the contrary, everywhere strength, and "the purest Mozartian grace". Grace that reflects on Genoa and makes this city even more cherished. There is now a real frenzy of walks, especially since prolonged reading always brings on intolerable headaches. He discovers a new garden, *his* garden, that of the Villetta Negro,[4] right by his lodgings. A place surely worthy of more than the praises Stendhal sang of it. Carmen, the garden of the Villetta Negro, the good, the beautiful: such are medicines.

Dawn was not a success, but *The Gay Science* would wreak vengeance, that bitter and exuberant book which taught that no knowledge exists, no single truth, and that life itself is only a form of death. For God, too, is dead. Nietzsche is not saying that God does not exist, but that he is dead. It is only a corpse which lies in the books of human superstitions. Nietzsche did not have a sense of fear towards God, because he did not have a sense of sin. This true Christian, a born Christian, if I may be so bold, is the one who has a true sense of sin. I catch the sense of a satanic reality, the awareness of the fight to be waged, the need to seize *his* devil by the throat. He who does not know possession cannot little care for a God who is totally ignorant of his struggles and defeats. Nietzsche's God is only the legislator of constellations, he has no access to the heart of man. He is so obscure in himself that the image of Satan is in vain. They are characters devoid of face or voice. In earlier ages, no doubt, in those naïve epochs of the world, they endured amongst us. But the discoveries of modern science and the meditations of philosophers have long since despatched them. They both perished under the gaze of knowledge.

A seismic event. Willed by the evil fatality that hangs over men, and perhaps disproportionate to their size. One would have to be God to comprehend its significance. Or at least a new Diogenes, in search of God, of a new God, capable of inventing a new suffering, since the acts of renunciation commanded by the Christian ideal are so easily obtained. And men would of course mock this lantern-bearer. They would even be in terror of him, for who would dare to recreate divine life knowing that God is dead? A man par excellence, a perfect man, teacher of a God far nobler, less bloodthirsty than the old: the truth. And here once more is announced at the pass of the high mountains the near and still-invisible Zarathustra.

While waiting to descend with the Tablets of future wisdom, Nietzsche is absorbed in the *Gay Science*, a festive book after the privations and sufferings (because for the first time he actually feels well), the jubilation felt at strength re-emerging, presentiment of the future, newly parting seas. A book in which we see Nietzsche, perhaps for the only time, properly young, powerfully happy. He truly sings in this book, entirely written over the month of January 1882. It is the beatitude of the convalescent, which all of us have known after long illnesses when our recovered strength fills us with faith in our talent, in our love. That moment when once more we could feel the world with our hands. Where the most insignificant bloom on our table opened up a whole future of triumphant holidaying. Convalescence is a like a subtler level of health which wishes to be conquered each day and, after the delays caused by the disease, pushes us blithely towards the future.

Heading for Messina on a small Italian sailing boat, Nietzsche endures a miserable crossing. Regardless, his joy remains undimmed. He rejects sketches of several new poems and disembarks in Sicily, that landmark of the world where, according to Homer, contentment dwells. A modest, quiet hotel, a place in the shade, palm trees.

> Calm, calm, remain calm!
> Know the weight of a palm
> Bearing its profusion!
> [...]
> Patience, patience
> Patience in the azure!
> Each atom of silence
> Is the chance of a ripe fruit!

Nietzsche lived by these lines by Valéry while writing his *Idylls from Messina*.[5] As he says somewhere, his heart had ascended to his brain. He took the chance to pluck its ripened fruit.

> From a torso branch I am here suspended,
> And I balance my weariness.

That speaks of yearning, the dancing minstrel, the Provençal. It was in Messina that Nietzsche began to dance his work and thought. Little did he know that a mere stone's throw away from him, in a hotel in Palermo, Wagner was putting the final touches to his own song in the tears of *Parsifal*.

Zarathustra actually appeared at this moment high up in the mountains. But he could not descend again amongst men until he had passed through the trial of love. Nietzsche sensed this, as he noted in the penultimate part of his *Gay Science*: "I feel disgust at my wisdom, like the bee that has gathered too much honey: I need hands that reach out." It was then that he received an invitation from Rome from Mlle de Meysenbug, his old friend. He left immediately to join her.

VI

Mlle Lou on Naxos

No sooner has he arrived than Nietzsche pays a visit to our "idealist" in Sorrento. Like many old maids who have mourned a fiancé all their lives, Malwida has a penchant for arranging weddings. And if she had urged Nietzsche so forcefully to come to Rome, it was because the idea that drove her was to marry off her wild young poet-philosopher with a young Russian of whom she had made herself the protector. Right from the off she sang her praises. She was Lou Salomé, Jewish and of Finnish descent.[1] Lou was only twenty years old, possessed of an understated beauty, a sprightly and rigorous intelligence, and wore the look of good fortune. Highly cultivated and entirely independent, the girl, raised in a liberated atmosphere, was seeking to enrich her leisure hours and would certainly ask for nothing better than to marry her expanding intellect to the destiny of the wandering professor whose name was just beginning to shimmer in the wider world. Lou had been initiated into Nietzsche's works by Meysenbug and her friend Paul Rée, who was also passing through Rome. It wasn't long before Lou showed an interest. It was not even concealed from Nietzsche that this tender disciple already had a teacher and special friend in Helsinki, in the person of an eminent professor who was, however, married and absorbed in his academic duties. Courageously, she had exiled herself. Thus she found herself in Rome in search of an affection which, without demanding anything from her pained heart, could at least occupy her mind. These traits did not displease Nietzsche and he willingly consented to see her. So, one fine day in late April, the Antichrist and the young Jewish woman were introduced to each other in St Peter's Basilica.

Lou was captivated. If Nietzsche, true to his theories, wore the mask of conventional politeness, she soon saw that he wore it badly. His gaze betrayed him, that myopic gaze which never reflected the changing impressions of the outside world but revealed interior horizons in a kind of luminous fixity. These luminosities struck her, enthralled her. As for Nietzsche, he was smitten right away and quickly on his guard. Writing to his sister, he judged Mlle Salomé not overly attractive and perhaps lacking personality, yet retracted this later in the very same letter and let slip that he was won over: "A young woman who from her earliest childhood sought only knowledge and made every sacrifice to acquire it. This moved me deeply." To Malwida Meysenbug, he said: "Here is a soul which, with one breath, has created a little body for itself." Nietzsche could scarcely believe the happiness he experienced from feelings of love. And there is no doubt: he loved. And with that marvellous injustice of the just, who have an absolute idea of perfection. With that superb egoism of lovers which he himself had sung of as the ferocious and necessary ideal of possession. The two enjoyed long conversations together which left them both in a state of restiveness: Lou, from the violence of Nietzsche's thought, his solemnly whispered words, his over-intelligent hands which still betrayed him, even from those ears "made to hear what has never been said". Nietzsche, moved by an intellect and feminine presence which the years of solitude had long deprived him.

They set off for Lake Orta, the four of them, Mme Salomé, her daughter Lou and the two philosophers. Nietzsche declared to Rée: "She is a truly admirable woman, you should marry her." And the other replied: "Marry her yourself, she is the very companion you need." They larked around like children, pushing Lou in a gardener's wheelbarrow,[2] as she decided to "sacrifice her life for truth". Nietzsche closely studied this young woman of precocious intelligence, who possessed such an impressive foundation of knowledge.

They parted, only to meet again a few days later, in the middle of May, in Lucerne. It was certainly Nietzsche who chose the meeting place. With a new feeling that filled him with a grateful gentleness, he wished to pay homage to his past. What past? The friendship with Wagner? The unexpressed—inexpressible—love for Cosima? Whatever the case, he was of a mind to take Lou to Tribschen, that blessed isle, that Naxos where Wagner and Cosima had once lived hours so replete with faith and enthusiasm. But first he instructed Rée to give the young woman a letter which contained a marriage proposal. "Because," he gently enquired of his friend, "of course there exists the possibility of a free union?" The naivety of the scholar and artist who hardly dwells in eventualities. In any case, Mlle Salomé was of too practical a mind and did not feel sufficient love to even consider such a hypothesis. Nietzsche's abrupt approach surprised her. She didn't quite believe it, or didn't want to believe it. Would she have preferred to become engaged to

Rée? Maybe. Whatever the case, it seems certain that in spite of a strong sympathy of spirit and undisguised admiration for Nietzsche's intellect, she was not in love with Nietzsche. Genius—and even talent—often finds it difficult to locate the path to the heart, for instincts rise up against this subtle enemy of its demands. Do we forgive intelligence, if we believe it to be incapable of failing? Lou was insightful, as any woman is when it comes to the deepest truths of flesh and blood. She saw clearly the danger such a man presented, and thus countered with a convenient lie. It was agreed with Rée that, for lack of an opportune moment, the letter had never been delivered. They gained a few more days and departed for Tribschen.

Nietzsche had first visited Tribschen on the 15th May 1869, the Saturday before Pentecost. As a young professor at the University of Basel, he had written to Wagner expounding his enthusiasm for his music, and he felt moved by this man as by a supernatural, divine being, one "possessed". And now the master had summoned him directly, and Nietzsche stood rooted before the gate of the villa where the eternal exile had sought refuge, hearing only the beating of his heart. He also heard a pained chord pushed down hard, struck over and again and leaking from an open window into the spring garden. A servant soon came to inform him that his master would work on till two o'clock and would not be able to receive the professor until after that time. Finding the wait intolerable, Nietzsche turned and left. All he took away from this first attempt was this one chord, endlessly repeated, which had descended to die amongst the flowers like a distant call, a weary questioning. Later, he was to recognize it in the passage from the third act of *Siegfried*, where Brunhild exclaims: "He wounded me, the one who awakened me…", and espy in it a rather surprising portent. He then returned to Tribschen on Pentecost Monday, and this time was received by the composer and Cosima von Bülow. So commenced the passionate friendship, the joyful and brief period when his uncritical heart accepted the intrusion of the most violent thought of its era.

"My Italy," said Nietzsche of this sunny peninsula on Lake Lucerne, at the end of which stood the shelter which the King of Bavaria had rented to his illustrious friend. Nietzsche travelled there from Basel almost every Saturday, spending the night and on Sunday counting the days which separated him from the next visit. And, as if this new friendship must right away give rise to extraordinary events, Nietzsche's first stay was marked by the birth of the son of Wagner and Cosima; then, a few weeks later, his visit coincided with the birth of the other Siegfried, the spiritual son of the master. Wagner worked tirelessly on his music, trying to reveal in it a philosophical expression. Beside him, Nietzsche worked no less strenuously, aroused by the Dionysian enthusiasm of this music, and the certainty of being the first to properly scrutinize all the composer's intentions, perhaps to grasp their meaning at a more profound level than even him. Already from this dawning, a presentiment came to him of a possible intellectual error made by his guide and the proud assurance of his own superiority in culture and divination. Between these two passionate revolutionaries stood Cosima Liszt.

How she seduced Nietzsche, this haughty young aristocratic woman of thirty-two years, who sacrificed the affection of her father, the marital bond which still bound her to Hans von

Bülow, the respect of the world, official virtues and the social tranquillity to the glory of the fifty-year-old Saxon, who rolled on from exile to exile, his worn-out travelling trunks stuffed with unplayable dramas! If the proximity of genius was for Nietzsche a splendid motive for spiritual exaltation, something quite else and more profound was created by the presence of this most feminine and secret being, of this voluntary and supple intelligence, this "sole woman of superior style" that he had yet known. Doubtless, he sought Wagner's endorsement in writing his *Birth of Tragedy*; but still more the admiration of this high-flown lover, of whom he had fashioned, in the most hidden depths of his heart, the ideal of the Dionysian maenad. Musing on her, he found only one name, the one which seemed symbolically destined for her like the woman abandoned by Theseus: Ariadne.[3] This Lucerne peninsula might as well have been Naxos. And he, Nietzsche, its labyrinth. Or Dionysus himself.

Some thirteen years before that spring day of 1882, it was not the young woman that Nietzsche was escorting through these lanes, but the enigmatic Ariadne. Piercing, sweet, wretched memories. In front of them walked Elisabeth Nietzsche, his sister, alongside Wagner in velvet jacket, knee-length breeches and black stockings, with his famous chef's hat and pale-blue cravat. Then came Ariadne and Nietzsche. She was wearing a pink cashmere dress with a wide lace collar. From her arm hung a large Florentine hat trimmed with flowers. They walked close together and often in silence. How sublime those silences! How charged with the inexpressible! And when they finally began to speak, all seemed so natural and perfectly tuned to their souls, these thoughts on Greek tragedy through which they entered, as if on steps of marble, into the human tragedy. Besides, wasn't she three-quarters Latin, this Frenchwoman born on Lake Como and raised wholly in Paris? Such delicate, subtle reason she had, to capture these "Mediterranean" nuances by which her own ideas already took on those of Richard, but with a far lighter air. It was he, Friedrich Nietzsche (who claimed to be a descendant of Polish nobility), who was the ideal lover of this high-born great lady, rather than this common labourer in Saxon music. That he was a man of power and even brilliance was not in doubt. But wasn't he somewhat lacking that refinement of spirit and manners that makes a woman of substance look for far more in the man she loves than over-exalted and perhaps now lapsed accomplishments? Cosima must have harboured a taste for the lights and shadows which envelop genuine spiritual heights and are naturally of an altogether different quality, rather than the crude lighting of the theatre stage. But she gave away nothing of her reflections. Any more than Nietzsche. They walked in concert, often spent whole days together, brushing against each other's souls with the antennae of the spirit. And yet how natural and simple she also knew to be, this so distant-seeming woman! She loved to laugh, joked light-heartedly, played with her children, ordered Nietzsche to shop for a Christmas tree, for books, dolls, puppets, asked for more pink-hued angels and a more satanic-looking devil. And for his trouble, Nietzsche received a fine bound edition of Montaigne's *Essays*. Wagner, moreover, entrusted his young friend with missions of confidence, leaving the proof-reading and printing of the master's autobiography in Basel to Nietzsche's care. This was to be printed in a dozen copies, for private individuals only. (And what discretion Nietzsche demonstrated right to the end, keeping all he knew of Wagner, his origins and birth, to himself.) It was then the time for the full measure of mutual confidence, February 1871. Squeezed into the little two-seater sleigh, Friedrich and Elisabeth slid under the bright winter sun, to the rhythm of the horse's bells, on the slopes that rise or fall amongst the fir trees quilted in silence and spangled with crystals, towards the antechamber of Italy.

Nietzsche recalls all this on the shores of this poignant lake. Or rather, he hears it once more; for it is never by the eye that he remembers (that too-myopic eye), but by the ear. His nostalgia does not concern the countries he has seen, the colours, the images, the faces, but the music he has heard there, the voice of the beings he loved, the sound of the air he breathed, the ground he trod, and ultimately the life of harmony, the song of things or of people. As with the blind, it is this immaterial matter which finds its way to the inner depths, and, on days sorrowfully mild with memory (like this day), rises from forgetting to populate the air, the shingle, the shore with painful resonances. Rarely, it seems to me, is the definition of melancholy advanced by Gide in his *Fruits of the Earth*[4] better exemplified than here, by this man and in this moment of poignant solitude: "Melancholy is only the afterglow of ardour."

So, his first work appeared at the beginning of 1872. Wagner wrote to him by return post: "I have never read anything more beautiful than your book…" And Cosima: "Your writing answers all the questions I was enquiring of my heart…" Then, later: "How beautiful your book is! How beautiful and profound! How profound and daring! Who will reward you for it, I would ask myself with some anxiety, if I did not know that, in the conception of these things, you must have already found the most beautiful reward. But if you feel rewarded, how do you know how to bring your inner, grandiose and constructive state of the soul into harmony with the outside world in which you are obliged to live?

"You have in this book evoked demons that I imagined obedient to the master alone. In two worlds, one of which is invisible to us, because it is too far distant, and the other of which we cannot know since it is too close, you have cast the brightest clarity so that we can grasp the beauty whose presentiment so delighted us, and we understand better the ugliness under which we were all but crushed. Your light, for our comfort, you project into the future—which is a gift for our heart—so that we can, full of hope, say this prayer: May the good be triumphant.

"I cannot tell you how much your book, in which you observe with such genuine simplicity the tragedy of our existence, seemed to me of a nature to uplift thought… I read these writings as if a poem, which however opens up the deepest problems; and I cannot part with it, nor the master, because it provides a response to all the unconscious questions of my soul…"

All intellectual Germany is stirred up, exclaims, and takes sides for or against this bold newcomer who proclaims in Wagner the birth of the new art. And beneath this aesthetic war, which, for years to come, will turn the music world of Europe upside down, another drama is emerging, this bewildering paradox which will see Wagner's Saint John the Baptist soon become his Judas. For Nietzsche still feels an intolerable disturbance. And his violence—he is quite aware—will become worse and worse because so much love, so many disillusions can only lead to increased opposition, each eternally eager to justify themselves. But Bayreuth is nonetheless partly his work. He was, along with Liszt, one of the two prophets. And the dawn rising there now in the Bayreuth Festival Theatre, he feels an instinctive loathing for it, without daring to admit it, since it will bring about the twilight of Tribschen.

Six more months, the last six months. The visits are ever closer. He counts them: twenty-three in all, over these three years. The time is approaching for a farewell to this little patch of blessed land. Now the last Easter holidays: they hide eggs to amuse the children; they present each other with little gifts; they still walk together in this supreme and too-honeyed spring and on those same paths where now this young foreigner is listening without a word to Nietzsche's protracted and uneven monologue.

Finally, the last day arrives, which is also the last Saturday in April. Wagner has already settled in Bayreuth and Cosima is preparing to leave for ever the house she occupied for seven years, where her son was born, where so many glorious pages were written, where she has known alongside, as if on the margin of the personal admiration she devotes to the great ageing man, this young professor, so modest, so discreet, and yet she guesses everything, quivering with a dominating tenderness. Who knows what complaints, what intellectual vexations will not one day erupt from this ingenuous soul, forced into too long a constraint! Because there is always a revenge of the heart. Who was a martyr may one day become a torturer. Even if his hatred is only indirectly aimed at the object of his resentment, the joy is no less powerful to see stagger, the one who remains ignorant of your strength. Of course, the match was not even, between the illustrious composer and the little professor who had barely emerged from the shadows. But the time will come—it must come—when Nietzsche will dare to compete with Wagner, when Dionysus will defeat Siegfried and can, head held high, claim the honour of knowing how to love.

This Saturday in April 1872 was therefore earmarked for an important farewell. Cosima and Nietzsche were busy amongst the trunks, in the unfurnished rooms, the ruins. The melancholy spread to the air and the clouds. The master's big, black Newfoundland refused all food. The servants were sobbing. Ariadne herself, so watchful over any expression of her feelings, betrayed her upset without even being aware. Nietzsche felt the urge to flee. The most lavish years of his young life had finally crumbled to dust. He now demanded an absolute silence, absolute self-possession. It was the other side of existence that suddenly emerged now before him. He then wrote to his friend Gersdorff—would he remember? "Do not bear a grudge if I leave a great fermata in our correspondence…"

Ten years of this sort of thing. And now, in that month of May 1882, what had happened to that Naxos deserted by the Gods?

The house was occupied by strangers. The two walked around the garden, sat by the lake. Ah! Sad and beautiful lakes, who know with your tender silences how so forcefully to reopen our wounds! Nietzsche fell silent for a long time, after an equally long speech, and dived into his recollections. ("Memory is a festering wound," he would soon write). Then he declared how much he had suffered at the hands of Wagner and his art. He revealed the price of sacrifice he had paid to find himself, since this gradual conquest had cost him the joy of youth. He had lost his health too, as if the gods wished to punish him for his denial. His intellectual anxiety, his sicknesses, his loneliness, everything dated from that cruel time when he had to detach himself from innocent beliefs and enter the morbid but liberating era of self-knowledge. From birth to himself. This, perhaps, was the uncanny wound of the Valkyrie, blind or sleeping genius, awakened by Siegfried's keen sword. Mighty pain, which most men ignore since so few possess the courage to meet such hard conquests. And now he was consecrating his life to it. And this consecration would be tantamount to suicide.

But could this Lou Salomé, sensitive as she was, properly grasp it? All that a tempestuous mind declaimed about such subjects must surely strike fear into any soul in search of wider contentment. Nietzsche remained silent. He had spoken in a low, contained voice, drawing in the sand with the tip of his cane, like Jesus writing on the ground before the adulterous woman. When he looked up he saw her eyes were welling with tears.

They parted company once again. Nietzsche travelled to Basel to his friends Professor Overbeck and his wife, from there to Tautenburg, in the forests of Thuringia. His sister Elisabeth, Paul Rée and Lou Salomé met nearby in Bayreuth, where the first performances of *Parsifal* took place at the end of July. Lou carried with her, as an antidote, the philosopher's essay entitled "Richard Wagner in Bayreuth", supplemented by recent notes. He hoped that, thanks to these corrections, she would be able to read between the lines of this old text and would come to learn that, in her most Wagnerian time, all her disillusions were already betrayed. Strange as it may sound, he was holding fast to this ordeal. Trial by fire. There is a particular pleasure for certain souls insatiable with pride, in provoking diabolical temptations in the object of their love with the hope of triumphing over them. To reach the core of Nietzsche's heart meant crossing the Wagnerian flame without being consumed by it. He himself now stood beyond that fiery zone, like the sword behind the dragon, the spirit behind the senses.

Parsifal was hailed a victory. "Long live Cagliostro!" penned an enraged Nietzsche. "The old enchanter has had a sure-fire success; the old gentlemen were all weeping..." Once again Wagner barred the way, robbing him of the soul he cared most about. He was confused, and was of a mind that it would never return to him. Yet Lou and Elisabeth hastened to the hotel where Nietzsche was awaiting them. The day before her departure from Bayreuth, Elisabeth Nietzsche had conducted an interview with Wagner in which the latter, despite his triumph, seemed to her jaded. Perhaps he was seeking a rapprochement with his disciple, a reconciliation. But he must have known this was impossible. "Tell your brother," he said, "that since he deserted me I am completely alone." But Nietzsche had no wish to hear such a whispered appeal. Moreover, he immediately set about cleansing the young woman he loved. After the mystery of Christian pain it was necessary to understand the more sober tragedy of human pain. Accept the pain. Love pain, for it is our destiny and our life, because without it we are nothing. "What? A God who loves men but only on condition that they believe in him, this same God would cast the most terrible glances and threats upon those who have no faith in his love? How? A love with clauses, such would be the sentiment of an all-powerful God? A love that hasn't even mastered wounded pride and angry revenge? How terribly oriental all this is. 'What business is it of yours whether I love you?'—this on its own is a sufficient criticism of all Christianity." And besides, wasn't Lou Jewish? Pain and pleasure, these are the two chief wisdoms. "We immoralists."—"We people without a homeland."

Did she finally understand?

No, she did not understand. He tried to persuade himself that he despised her. He was jealous. She was flirting again with Rée and he loathed their intimacy. Once more he fell ill, sent her notes from room to room. "In bed. Dreadful attack. I cannot bear life." Forgetting how much he had exalted her and the honours granted to suffering.

On 13th July, he had written to Peter Gast: "This young woman has the piercing gaze of an eagle and the courage of a lion...", but on 4th August: "A bird has flown by, it was not an eagle."

Mlle Salomé composed a poem, "To Pain", and Nietzsche was transported. Then a "Hymn to Life", which directly inspired the musical interpretation of which we have already spoken. We must hear it a few times before daring to state that it is Wagnerian. But this is a fact. And what must Nietzsche have thought when he received from Gast, in response to this sending, these lines: "Your music makes a Christian sound. If you had sent me the music without a text, I would have believed it was a march for the crusaders—belligerent in a Christian manner." Christian and Wagnerian, such was the musical soul of Nietzsche, which, without any of the "repentance" of the spirit, expressed what for him was inexpressible.

What he had composed in his childhood showed echoes of the Wagnerian. The oratorio from his thirteenth year, for example, has a key with a notably "Parsifalesque" expression. On coming upon it in his papers, he was terrified to find there the secret kinship which linked him to Wagner. But isn't this logical? Finding himself so close to him in terms of sensitivity, his critical intelligence foundered. He was one of those for whom denying and renouncing is a nervous necessity, the only way to assert oneself before oneself. Lay the blame on them, what does it matter. When poor Meysenbug implored Nietzsche to come back into the fold of Schopenhauer and Wagner, he smiled in pity. When his publisher suggested that he undertake something more "human", more suited "for the public", he was outraged and merely redoubled his efforts to take the lonely road.

Nietzsche did not live in sin, let's stress that. Like so many great rebels, he was pure. And like so many of the pure, he had a Christian heart. Do we not already see that he lived only for others, for their intellectual salvation? Perfection, to his mind, is the truth. His fidelity is offered to the spirit, his renouncements to knowledge. Like the greatest of the Christian saints, he, too, is a Patriarch of Poverty. I look at him, tormented by physical suffering, isolated in his spiritual belief, passionate about the happiness of men, and convince myself that he is in fact a sublime example of those whom Jesus calls the servants of God. If the kingdom of God is a state of joy, made up of all our sacrifices, who has possessed it better, after Francis of Assisi, than Nietzsche? And let us see, finally, that at the extreme point of this new bitterness, at the height of its disillusionment, the most beautiful fruit of pain will burst forth in life: a perfect work of art.

Did little Lou betray him? The word is too strong for anyone who has not loved. In any case, it seems that Rée had become dearer to her and Nietzsche ever more alienating. They parted ways again, then met in the autumn for a few days in Leipzig. The marriage proposal had been permanently postponed and tactfully declined. Elisabeth Nietzsche, who reviled the young

Russian, seems to have been behind the break-up which her brother sought as some kind of deliverance. Lou and Nietzsche parted, and each wrote the other letters that made it difficult to be reconciled. Nietzsche took up his pen one last time:

"What letters are yours, Lou! Worthy of those written by the little vindictive residents of a guest house. What am I to do with such miseries? Just try to understand me. I want you to feel greater when stood before me, not to diminish yourself further. How can I forgive you if I cannot first find in you the qualities for which you can be forgiven?... How impoverished you are in reverence, gratitude, piety, courtesy, admiration, delicacy—not to mention higher things.

"I have not been wrong about anyone yet: I have seen in you that sacred egoism which forces us to serve what is lofty in us. I cannot conceive by what helpful sorcerer's spell you have traded it for the opposite one, the egoism of the cat which desires only life...

"Goodbye, dear Lou, I won't see you again."

He immediately departed for Basel, and to his friends the Overbecks declared: "Today I enter into complete solitude." Mme Overbeck questioned him, for she sensed that he was emerging from a decisive crisis. She confided in him that she herself no longer found in religion either consolation or the possibility of fulfilment, that "the very notion of God simply does not hold enough real content for me". Nietzsche, visibly moved, replied: "You only say that to come to my aid. Never give up on this idea of God: you carry it unconsciously within you; for as you are, as I always find you, and until this very moment, a great idea governs your whole life, and that great idea is the idea of God."

The more he deprived himself, the more it seemed that he deemed it necessary to leave the nourishment for others who might still have the means to assimilate it. He added:

"As for me, I gave up this thought, I want to create something new, I have no right to go back. Because of my passions, I will sink, they will cast me here, now there: I keep losing my footing, but I don't care."

... "Don't go backwards", "Go further", "as far as possible", such are the mottos launched from Nietzsche's lips, taken up by Oscar Wilde, then by Gide, and where Charles Du Bos in his profound *Dialogue*[5] sees the prime temptation of our modern mind, "the peculiar form which the devil assumes in our time. It may well be true. But if such explorations in the moral or spiritual realm are only a trap set for human recklessness, let us view it as honourable to have at least set out on the adventure."

For Nietzsche, Italy alone could accept him, that radiant consoler, after these long months of impassioned misunderstandings. His soul lacked a skin, as he later said. He rediscovered Genoa, discovered Rapallo, Portofino, Zoagli. Around these gulfs, between these fishing villages and beneath the blue pines, you might see on his rounds he whom the Pharisees of ancient Judea could not have determined to be prophet or demon, the one whom the Genoese called *il piccolo santo*, and who carried wrapped in a towel a manuscript on which he had written in calligraphic letters: *Thus Spoke Zarathustra: A Book for All and For No One.*[6]

VII

Dead Gods and the Living Prophet

"We can only love what we create", says Valéry. And Mauriac counters thus: "We can only love the one who created us... What we create is, on the contrary, what we reject, that which is dead." These are the two diverging attitudes of the intellectual and the Christian. For the first, all happiness is in oneself or of oneself, all enjoyment, all life. For the other, man measures his worth by his power to again become the child of a love a hundred times more magnanimous than his own. What the Christian gives is nothing but restitution, burning tears with which he waters his dear detestable sin. But the man of the mind feeds his pride, even when he delights in his disenchantments. A fundamental misunderstanding which will ever divide the highest souls. The kingdom of God is not of this world, says the one. And the other: you have to love this earth. A simple variant, moreover, of the old distinction established by Saint Paul in his letter to the Romans, between those who worshipped and served the Creature over the Creator.

The stems of human poetry, despite such variances, nevertheless merge at the root. It is from the same heart that they spring forth, the same sap with which they nourish themselves. But how different are the flowers and the fruits. Who will decide their taste, their beauty? Jesus and Zarathustra? Let us rule out any impiety here. We are not trying to see man as equal to God; but on the contrary, to understand why one alone brings us in its lyrical richness a rare fruit of bitter flavour; the other, the humble wheat ear of a peasant, but heavily laden with all human harvests. Millions reread the Gospels, a few hundred at best reread Zarathustra. So, does the bearer of sufferings attract more powerfully than the taker of joys? Zarathustra desires to dance his life, dance God. He exalts the will to power. He creates the moral of the masters. The paradise of Jesus is open only to slaves, to the weak, to the suffering. The morality of the vanquished and the failing, says Nietzsche. God is only interested in the lost sheep, Nietzsche only in the wise but daring sheep, in the one who, far from slipping into the abyss, ascends to the heights.

You have to choose between the strong and the weak, and humanity instinctively tends towards the weak. The weak are full of illusions and promises. Weakness attracts with its mystery, its shadow, its possibilities, its impossibilities. "There are preachers of death, and the world is crowded with those to whom it is necessary to preach that they turn away from life… They are drawn out of life by the lure of eternal life." They are the consumptives of the soul. These are the so-called good ones. These are the chaste. How to explain: the chaste through ignorance; the good ones by lack of critical sense; lovers who forget the true law of all love: its egoism.

However, Zarathustra teaches the love of life, not that of death. He teaches the love of the furthest, not that of the neighbour. Show us, he said, that you are one of those who covet. That you are one of those who have firmly planted *their* good and *their* evil, that you don't flee the yoke, but wilfully assume your own. Be alert to the good and the righteous. Be alert to holy simplicity. He said to the women: May there be valour in your love. May it be your honour to always love more than you are loved. He also tells that love is not philanthropy. It is often just one animal who recognizes another.

Jesus died too young, and the Hebrews are sorrowful in their youth. Jesus never had time to laugh. He didn't have time to recant. The love of a young man lacks experience and maturity; that is why he is contemptuous of men and the earth. But never forget, it is this life, your life, which is eternal life.

So speaks Zarathustra in his first book. And, having spoken thus, he said, like Gide in his *Nourritures*: "Now I order you to lose me and find yourselves."

It was completed in ten days, from the 1st to the 10th of February 1883, this first book Nietzsche writes under the dictation of his voices, without any hesitation, almost without a single crossing out, and in a rapture that sometimes brings him to tears. But under a certain pressure as well. "I never had a choice," he says. In the morning he walks south, on the picturesque road which climbs towards Zoagli and its heights in the pine woods. In the afternoon he walks around the bay of Santa Margherita, behind Portofino. These are his paths, his roads to Damascus, this is the land of his visions. It was here that Zarathustra was revealed to him, that Nietzsche was "overwhelmed" by him. Nietzsche feels as light as a man who can now die without regret, he who had feared for so long that he could not sustain the health required for his task. Little strength does not give rise to great works. But nature almost always grants artists sufficient time to fully express themselves. Their vitality is secretly related to their work. Beethoven did not die until after the Ninth Symphony, and if Baudelaire, Rimbaud, Bizet and Chopin died before their time, it is undoubtedly because they had sung their song.

Nietzsche is flooded with forebodings. His father died at the age of thirty-six and there is a physiological mystery in the parallelism of longevity between a father and his children. The time of Zarathustra is precisely that when Nietzsche traverses the critical age of the males in his family, and he feels the thermometer of vitality dropping within him. "At the same age as him," he wrote to Gast, "I reached the very lowest point… I have now reached the years when my father died…" Had he not sung his poem too, how would he find a means to go on, a new reason for living? He was going to discover how, though, and in a most unexpected way.

On 14th February, on returning to Genoa, Nietzsche opened the newspaper and saw the announcement of Wagner's death. The very day his old god (another dead god!) disappeared, he created the new god. A magnificent subject of exaltation. "In the same sacred hour," he wrote. We can see how the torch is passed on. Reaching for his pen right away, he wrote to Cosima: "Not what you lose, but what you now possess, I see it stood before my soul… I look towards you as towards the most honoured woman of my heart."

Essentially, Nietzsche feels delivered by this illustrious corpse. "It is hard," he told Gast, "to have to be the enemy of the one you venerated most for six years… But it was against the *old* Wagner that I had to defend myself. As far as the *real* Wagner is concerned, it is I who am foremost his heir." By which he did not mean the heir of his thought, but assuredly of his grandeur, of his Dionysian rhythm. A sort of sacred delirium. But as he is fond of restating: the true artist is one who is delirious reasonably. Now, since it is a question of reason, why would he refuse to see what Wagner was for him, to do justice if not to the work, then at least to the man? He had loved him, and strongly. "It was truly," he says, "a love without ulterior motive," and he muses dejectedly of the time when he heard the birth of that final part of *Siegfried*... Times long passed, however, and more so since the birth of his beloved child, his Zarathustra. And, still in the same trance of excitation, he announces to his publisher a fifth gospel, "something for which there is no name as yet, by far the most serious of my testimonies". He asks for this dithyrambic poem a garment worthy of him, the finest vellum, and each page framed.

With that: music, Bizet, Carmen, travel propositions. Will it be Barcelona or Courmayeur, at the foot of Mont Blanc? It was Rome. Rome, Piazza Barberini no. 56, *ultimo piano*, with the Swiss landscape painter Muller. The Eternal City is a detestable city for Nietzsche. It weighs on his mind with all its churches, all that Roman marble. Barbarian heaviness on his Greek heart. Before the Basilica of Constantine he exclaims: "That there is struggle and inequality even in beauty, war for power and for superpower, is what we are instructed here in the clearest allegory." However, refrains still sing within him. "Death by immortality", for instance. Thought where time disperses like a vapour, where philosophy takes on its most expansive meaning. He composed his "Night Song",[1] which he blended with the second book of *Zarathustra*, with the sound of the Triton Fountain in Piazza Barberini and the shadow of amorous couples lengthening over the cobbles. Solitary in his loggia, his high perch, Nietzsche watches and listens. "My poverty, that my hand never ceases giving; my jealousy is to see eyes filled with expectation and nights illuminated by desire." She is already faded now, erased from memory, little Lou. Sometimes he wonders whether he was not prey to a hallucination. No, his heart is still pained. But is it not rather our suffering that we regret when we regret love, a suffering by dint of being felt and caressed, almost amounting to joy? The "bittersweet", as our poets of the sixteenth century had it, this is the sap that nourished Zarathustra's second book. It is sensually and almost lovingly that Nietzsche now articulates his suffering, his suffering lived, appreciated, overcome.

"Now," said Christ to Peter, "now you are girding yourself and going where you wish to go..."

Neither mistress, nor disciple, nor friend. How Nietzsche must have understood the means to harden the loneliness all about him! Those hours of failure and abandonment when we befriend anyone, a waiter or a working girl, these he has never known. Those sluggish hours when, before the rising flood of despondency, a little beauty and youth is a lifeline to us, he was indifferent to them. (One night, in Toulon, I saw a refined young woman enter some den of iniquity and seize the arm of a little sailor just to press a measure of her loneliness into those placid muscles. Immediate appeasement, spreading across the mind.) But Nietzsche never needed anyone. He spoke for the deaf, enlightened only the blind and was never discouraged. What conviction he must have possessed, to go on with this frenzy of preaching, without followers and without hope! He yearned to give men new faith, joy and a reason to live. He showered the German people with poetry that rejuvenated their language. He invented an unknown verbal music ("I believe, with this *Zarathustra*, to have brought the German language to its perfection. After Luther and Goethe there remained a third step to be taken… my style is a dance, a game of symmetries of all kinds, a leap over these symmetries and their mockery… it goes as far as the choice of vowels.") To France he paid spiritual homage as the most penetrating critic of his time. He liberated souls—at least he believed so—from the most dangerous prejudices. But no one heard him. Only the Danish critic Georg Brandes[2] descended with a quiver of curiosity into this valley humming with the cries of new gods. And the old bourgeois Taine courteously sent his business card to this prince of the spirit. No doubt he must have taken him for some frustrated schoolmaster whose literary efforts were undervalued.

Departing Rome, Nietzsche headed to the Engadine to write, and in a mere ten days the second book of *Zarathustra* appeared. There he still left an image of Lou Salomé, dancing not with the head of a new Saint John the Baptist, but with Love.

"I am only variable and wild, and a woman in everything. I am not a virtuous woman, though for you men I am *the infinite, or the faithful, the eternal, the mysterious.*

"But you other men, you always lend us your own virtues, alas! Virtuous as you are!"

Indeed, how absurd it seems to us, our virtue, in the face of the admirable nature of woman, which always expresses the exacting truth that roots her to the earth: her desire.

On the hunt again into the wind, the hard ground, the rock, the pines creaking with drought in the sun, on towards the horizon—ever the same—the Mediterranean horizon.

*

Nice, the end of 1883 and into January 1884.

The mistral, the Provençal, everything jangling, whistling, both light and strong in the way of the spirit. Nietzsche has settled in the old town, close to the port. And as is his custom he walks, his cane striking the cobblestones or the rough pebbles of the outer roads. After weeks of fresh suffering, such that he fears he is on the verge of going insane and sliding into suicide, suddenly there is an unexpected convalescence, akin to a resurrection, a blossoming. He discovers Èze, a Moorish village in the direction of Monaco, perched atop its old African rock. And in the third book of *Zarathustra*, the harsh wind blows in his ear from the branches of olive trees. "I am a traveller and a mountain climber," he says to his heart. "Always love your neighbour as yourself, but be first of those who love themselves—who love themselves with great love, with great contempt. Thus spoke the impious Zarathustra."

It is on these Spanish walls, before this Italian blue and in this light rustle of French foliage, that Nietzsche created the very soul of his pagan Christ: the chapter "On the Ancients and the New Tables".

"When I came upon men, I found them seated on an old assumption. For a long time, they all believed that they knew what is good and what is bad for humankind…"

"This is also where on my way I picked up the word superhuman, and this doctrine: man is something that must be overcome…"

Yes, this is where Nietzsche knew best that he had overcome himself. Here he was as he wished to be, both the poorest and the richest. *Zarathustra* is his intimate book of edification, the reservoir of his courage. It is a poem sprung from the unconscious, from this unconscious that he considers so much more abundant than his conscious. In addition, all his works were born of forces to which he submitted, rather than orienting them himself. They have always become other than he wanted them to be. For such is the power of the unconscious that it still manages to make its way into form, into life. The role of the poet is to place the Pythia on his tripod, but whatever she says must be let go. Here, then, is the last prophet of intellectual Europe, so dead to lyricism with the war. His itinerary, from Sorrento to Venice, from Genoa to Portofino, from Sils Maria to Èze, a brief stop, later, in Turin, marks the final journey of the spiritual poet. We can follow it in three stages: acquire the knowledge of solitude and poverty; love existence even with disdain; reveal to the handful of worthy beings the ideal of the superhuman. Tasks by no means out of date, but rendered virtually impossible today, when life is no longer intended to be understood, merely lived.

Whoever ascends to Èze today, in 1929, no longer takes the stony paths the philosopher climbed in 1884, but travels by car via the Nouvelle Corniche; softly, pneumatically, not harshly, in hobnailed boots. He will glance distractedly at the poor Moorish walls. He will be more interested in the splendid villa-convent, "restored" by Mme Balsan, née Vanderbilt.[3] The dust of thought in the North, and in the South, fresh roses bounding with life. They have an easy victory in the abstract, these American roses. How Nietzsche would have endorsed them. Remain faithful to the earth, he would have warned us, even if you don't know why; simply because it is beautiful.

VIII

He Leaves a Country
Inhabited by No One

How he has a taste for the open air! "This is my most beautiful work room, this Piazza San Marco," Nietzsche wrote in April 1885. The beach and the pines of Sorrento, the ancient fortifications of Genoa, the gulf of Rapallo, the firs of Sils Maria, the paths that climb to Èze, and finally the precious Piazza San Marco, these make up his libraries. They prove more inspiring work rooms than those of professors. Though he still had in his room in Italy a few cases of books, a notepad and pen, sufficient for those who know how to look, how to listen, and draw their knowledge and music out from themselves.

Then there is the music of Peter Gast. No life is possible without music. Boon companions, there are none amongst those "melancholic and mad souls" profound enough and joyful enough that they cannot do without it. Amongst the living: Gast; amongst the dead: Stendhal and Abbé Galiani,[1] for one would not have existed without Cimarosa[2] and Mozart, the other without Piccinni.[3] Venice, for Nietzsche, is silence and a friend's piano. Alas! His poor eyes. Virtually blind now; veils over the pupils; tears beneath the eyelids; headaches always. But Venice remains Venice, a perfect city for meditation, and each evening Gast returns to the keyboard. Dear Gast, he is no more successful than Nietzsche in courting success. His opera is completed, but no theatre will agree to take it on. Yet, in Nietzsche's view, this is the finest work which has been accomplished in Germany since Mozart and Beethoven. And the philosopher exclaims:

"Wagneria is blocking your way, as well as this coarseness, this German thickness, which ever since the Empire has been increasing, ever increasing. We shall have to reach a decision and take up arms to prevent our being silenced, you and I..."

A forceful complaint, this "to die of silence"; though without grandiloquence, and how right and yet terrible to hear. For Nietzsche, in this spring of 1885, has the three parts of *Zarathustra* behind him, and all published, though (like every previous book) it has immediately come up against mute indifference. So much so that no publisher could be persuaded to print the fourth. He was obliged to bear the cost of the tiny print run of forty copies himself. Around ten volumes have been despatched to friends, and the remainder await readers worthy of the text. "I will be famous in forty years," he told the residents of the little hotel in Nice, who glanced knowingly at each other, barely concealing a smile. Stendhal, too, had said this, and for Stendhal it was beginning to hold true, but for Nietzsche? In forty years he would be eighty years old. He was the one to smile now, no, it wouldn't take that long. Maybe in two or three years? And anyway, he was still writing. He also made a short trip to Florence that year. I don't think he saw a single "work of art" there. He was now solely a man for the open air. But he went up to San Miniato[4] and gazed down on the city from above, like Dante, like Michelangelo, like all of us who have rooted on the terraces of that cemetery a memory that will accompany us until death. These are places at once too powerful and too gentle for us not to situate the face there on which all the beloved Florence of our heart is depicted. This beautiful eye which gazes at the dome in its mist, this mouth which smiles on the most tender city in Italy, this is our San Miniato and the poetry of our Tuscan mornings.

And Nietzsche, what of his encounter? With an old astronomer from the Arcetri Observatory, Leberecht Tempel, a German deeply attached to these heights who had read all his books and could quote many long passages from memory. Here is an author's happiness, if you will, in confessing to the pleasure gained from being read. Perhaps even a measure of emotion grazes this unrecognized friendship. In an existence like that of Nietzsche, this moment is worth noting, however insubstantial in terms of feeling it may seem to us.

When he returned to Venice the following spring (1886), Nietzsche brought with him a new completed manuscript, wrapped in paper and bound with little ribbons. It was *Beyond Good and Evil*,[5] which will stand as one of the purest-cut of his jewels, the most transparent of German prose. It is a truly astonishing work, and in philosophical terms magnificent that the more Nietzsche descends towards the extinction of his brain, the more his thought takes wing. There is now in him a gift of prescience, of divination, something almost supernatural. Bergson and Freud can be seen in the making on so many pages of his new book. Gide, too, even Maurras,[6] through the mouths of Machiavelli and Mussolini. Many of the problems of psychiatry, psychology and politics which light up our time are here raised and partially resolved in the sense of our present experience. Yet this book is directed against modernism. "It is a school for gentlemen", a focus on the distance between humans, between masters and slaves, between "progressives" and "vegetants". A classification of values. In short, a paean to heroes, not those officially recognized and petrified as statues, but heroes of the spirit, even though they remained fundamentally unknown all their lives like Nietzsche himself. Napoleon and Goethe, no doubt. But also Chopin and Proust. There is even a predilection in Nietzsche for the modest, the misunderstood, the self-effacing, the sick, his brothers. To him they seem more dignified, more elegant. This is a book about the culture of the heart as well as of the mind; a genealogy of consciousness and a natural history of morality. A table of hierarchies.

Do you prefer to be "master" or "slave"? Let's opt for master. So then, have the courage to clear out as many old tunes from your little souls as possible: equal rights—pity for all who suffer—kindness—altruism—otherwise, remain slaves. Are you one of those who wish to see the "plant of man" grow vigorously? You should have the genius of invention and concealment, a sense of constraint, the craving to exalt yourself to the will to power. For thousands of years we have been used to no longer considering the consequences of an act as decisive from the point of view of its value, but only its origin, its moral intention. "We immoralists" admit that it is no longer this origin that concerns us but its consequences. We are entering an extra-moral era.

"Where to direct our gaze? Towards new philosophers, towards minds strong enough and bold enough to provoke opposing judgements, to transform and overthrow 'eternal values'; towards the forerunners, towards the men of the future who, in the present, find the means to force the will of millennia to enter into new paths. To teach man that his future is his will, that it concerns a human will which prepares the great strivings and general trials of discipline and education, to put an end to this appalling domination of the absurd and of chance which until now has been called history—the idiocy of the greatest number is only its final form. To achieve this will one day require new philosophers and rulers, whose image will make all the hidden, terrible and benevolent spirits that have existed on this earth until now appear dull and parochial. It is the image of these leaders that floats before our eyes."

It is pertinent to note that these things were thought and written beneath the neighbouring sky to that under which, on that exact date, Mussolini was born. They are all steeped in Italy; both of an old Stendhal-type Italy and of a new, realistic young Italy; the Venice of a Peter Gast, with the resounding dancing music of a Georges Bizet. Here and there we spy again the phantom of Lou Salomé, whose dress Nietzsche grasps firmly as if about to tear it off: come, show us your pretty body of a wild animal, cunning female, your supple body of a cat on the prowl. But hold on, let me snip your claws first… there is a such a fulminating rage in his physiological examinations, such retrospective jealousy. This is the worst part, the most vengeful. "Men of deep sadness," he writes, "betray themselves when they are happy: they seize their happiness as if they wanted to embrace it and suffocate it with jealousy."

Suddenly, he decides to flee this peninsula which pains his eyes. He hurries straight to Leipzig in one go to see his friend Erwin Rohde, the Hellenist, to converse with someone of his rank, to explain himself. And Rohde, worried, will write: "His whole person was imbued with an indescribable strangeness... It seemed as if he had just come from a country where no one lives." This phrase is rather beautiful. Right away we sense the truth in it. Nietzsche came from a country where no one lives, where we are always alone, where we only encounter ourselves.

He takes his desperate, ecstatic, prophetic book to his publishers: "This is the music of the future," they say to him, smiling.

IX

All Problems Transposed in Feeling

Dionysian Dithyrambs

"Here are the songs of Zarathustra, as he sang them to himself, so that he could endure his last loneliness."

"The Fire Sign"

Here, where between seas an island arose,
An altar of stone towering up,
Here beneath the blackened sky,
Zarathustra lit his mountain fire,
The beacon for mariners adrift,
The question mark for those who have an answer...

This flame with a white-grey belly
Flickers its greedy flame into the cold distance,
Bends its neck towards ever purer heights—
A raised serpent of impatience,
This signal I placed before me.

86

My own soul is this flame:
Insatiable for new distances
Blaze upward, upward in silent passion.
Why did Zarathustra flee from animals and men?
Why did he run suddenly from all settled lands?
Six solitudes he knew already—
But the sea itself was not lonely enough for him,
The island let him rise, on the mountain he became flame,
Into a seventh solitude
Searching he casts now the hook over his head.

Lost mariners! Wreckage of ancient stars!
You seas of the future! Unexplored sky!
To all solitaries I now cast my hook:
Give an answer to the impatience of the flame,
Catch me, the fisherman on high mountains,
My seventh last solitude.

In September of the year 1886, the villagers of San Lorenzo and Camogli and the shepherds who lead their animals in the countryside around Portofino began to see, on the stony heights of this region, great fires of wood burning at dusk. No one knew which dogged and industrious tourist was climbing up there with dead branches to set them alight. It was Zarathustra sending out his last calls, launching his last signs into the distance. Or the mysterious walker who plunged into the valley of Christ, to the ruined monastery whose campanile sprang from the flowers like an old wall that a too-gentle death embraces. "You pay dearly to be immortal: you have to die several times while you are alive."[1] In search of an anti-Christian land, Nietzsche encountered these ruins of God everywhere. And he laughed silently. He was dead of Wagner, dead of Lou Salomé, dead of public incomprehension, dead of his friendships as well as his loves, and so he laughed knowing that he was immortal. Immortal from being alone and misunderstood. More immortal than Dante, Shakespeare and Goethe. This messianic madness took hold of him and pride swelled him like a balloon. "That a Goethe, a Shakespeare would not be able to breathe even for a moment in such an atmosphere of extreme fervour and dizzying altitude; that Dante, compared to Zarathustra, is only a believer and not one who first creates truth, a spirit that rules the world, a fatality; that the poets of the Vedas are priests, unworthy even to untie the cords of Zarathustra's sandals; all this is in the end no great thing and gives no inkling of the immeasurable distances of azure solitude in which this work dwells."

Finally, a man who dares to admit himself, who dares to write books without kindness and without "ideal", seeking only truth. The inventor not of an ideal, but of a counter-ideal. For Nietzsche discovered that pain alone unites us to life (but pain vanquished), and that intelligence is the only counter-poison to our despair. Great pain teaches great scepticism, and scepticism is the necessary antidote to nature's heady illusions. All the steps of his mind, his renunciations, his fatigue, his seventh loneliness, such are the works that had to be done to justify his last philosophy and to achieve a "trans-valuation of all values". The will to power is the glorified culmination which must be attained by anyone who seeks in this new dawn of the old world an honest reason for living.

Summarizing in a few words what he thinks, he, the "Good European", of all the cultures he has probed, ploughed, to try and germinate a unique new plant capable of rejuvenating and invigorating the ancient human vine.

He says:

"English genius makes all it receives coarser and more natural."

"French genius dilutes, simplifies, logicalizes, prepares."

"German genius entangles, transmits, confuses, moralizes."

"Italian genius is by far the one which makes the freest and most subtle use of what it has borrowed. It gives back a hundred times more than it receives, and is thus the richest genius, the one with the most to give."

And, moving on to a critique of "modernity", he sees there, forty years before us, all the signs that appear so obvious to us today: the exaggerated development of intermediary training, the withering away of types, the rupture of traditions, the predominance of instincts, the pre-eminence of traders, even *mercanti*, even in the intellectual field. Cast adrift by his friends and former masters, Nietzsche paradoxically feels stronger than ever. With that secret power that endows true creators with conviction of their right. Broken, perhaps, but all-conquering. The new prefaces he wrote in the autumn of 1886 for *Dawn* and *The Gay Science* are particularly inspiring and jubilant. He had returned from the far distance, from all malaise, from all truths, from all doubts. He saw now only a soft ironic light, the most delicate music in life itself, the universal smile of things. It was through weakness that he found himself strong. Through superiority, he became human once more. Through hardness towards himself, he knew himself to be the most tender of men.

An old lady from his pension, one of those sad, drifting wrecks that no wave ever carries into port, said to him:

"You write, Herr Nietzsche. I should like to know something of your books."

And since he saw she was devout:

"No," he replied, "I don't think so. If what I am printing is to be believed, a poor suffering creature like you would have no right to live."

He read the *Journal* of the Goncourts, became familiar with Sainte-Beuve, Flaubert, Gautier, Taine, Renan, Turgenev, and summarily declared them all pessimists, cynics, nihilists. In short, he recognizes them as so many kinsmen, yet they all lack this fundamental virtue: strength. He reads Baudelaire avidly. (Alas! A Wagnerian.) He enthusiastically discovers Dostoyevsky. "Do you know Dostoyevsky?" he asks Gast. "Save for Stendhal, no one has satisfied and enthralled me so much. Here is a psychologist for whom I truly have ears."

He confronts Wagner once more. For this is when Nietzsche hears *Parsifal* for the first and only time. Irresistibly attracted by the old Wagnerian enchantment, he travels to Monte Carlo where the orchestra has on its programme the prelude already celebrated across the concert halls of Europe. What need was he obeying, he who for more than ten years struggled against these feverish harmonies and wanted to hear only classically balanced music? We cannot know. Perhaps it was simply a question of sharpening up his forces of protest, of reinvigorating his combative powers by contact with this tragic decadent. Or perhaps, now that Wagner had sunk into the shadows, it was preferable to go and find him so as to prolong those silent discourses in which we give to the dead whom we have loved our rejoinders and our passions. Either way, Nietzsche was seized and almost subjugated.

"When I see you again, I want to tell you exactly what I came to understand," he wrote to Peter Gast on 21st January 1887. "Leaving aside all the inappropriate questions (what *can* such music be used for, what it *should* be used for), and if we adopt a purely aesthetic point of view, we can ask whether Wagner ever created anything better. The highest psychological awareness, in relation to what is to be said, is found expressed and *communicated* here; the shortest and most direct form of this conception; every nuance of feeling pushed to the epigram; a precision of music as descriptive art, which calls to mind an insignia worked in relief; and, ultimately, a sublime and extraordinary feeling, an event of the soul, placed at the foundation of the music. From this Wagner can draw the greatest honour; a synthesis of emotions which, to many men, even superior men, might seem incompatible; a judicial severity, an 'elevation' in the most terrifying sense of the word, an understanding and a penetration that cuts the soul like a knife—and once again: compassion for what the artist sees and judges. There are similar things in Dante, and nowhere else. Has a painter ever painted a look of love as melancholy as Wagner, with the final accents of his prelude?"

And around these words of Nietzsche's, what nostalgia, what regrets for the man from whom it was necessary, for the honour of the spirit, to part; but whose secret presence remains essential and irreplaceable in spite of all... If Wagner had felt alone after Nietzsche's defection, it is certain that Nietzsche could never fill the place in his heart that Wagner knew to be cavernous.

We are in the autumn of 1887. He is staying on Lake Maggiore; moves up to the Engadine; writes *On the Genealogy of Morals;*[2] then journeys down to Venice. It is no longer the cheerful Easter Venice of former years, the Venice of spring, a large marine shell resounding with bells and the intimate harmonies of Chopin and Gast; the blessed city, which has taught him so much about his own music, so many rhythmic secrets and sequences of sentences. The Venice of that autumn was a Venice of long walks and industrious note-taking. He gathers his strength with a view to his will to power. Gast looks on anxiously at his master, who is now three-quarters blind, seated for long hours on the terraces of the most undistinguished cafés, absorbed in his thoughts, dreadfully alone, tragic. Will he be granted the time to achieve the culmination of his work? Will he write his *Parsifal*? Wagner died just over there, a stone's throw away, on the Grand Canal. And Nietzsche, will he not fall, struck down, "dead of silence" before he can cut his veins to donate his purest blood? One can only think of all those illustrious ones who came there over centuries and seated themselves at the *gelati* vendors of Piazza San Marco: these poets, musicians, these lovers, these millionaires of life. One can hardly imagine that here, in this destitute and correct little philosopher—correct as genius, as Baudelaire might say—even something of the dandy, but shabby, not so handsome, living an invisible life. Yet he had never felt so weary, so fatigued. It's a sincere case of "decadence". Not an echo of his cries is sent out across the wider world. His only consolation is still music, because perhaps, deep down, he is nothing more than an old amateur musician. One day he confides in Gast that this was his true vocation, and that if he had written books, it was only "for want of anything better". And who are his readers? Mostly musicians: Mottl the conductor, Bülow, Brahms, Gast; a few rare professors and last friends: Rohde, Overbeck, perhaps Burckhardt. If he was to do the arithmetic, this is what he would find: at forty-three, he has written fifteen volumes, most of which were published at his own expense; he has hardly ever received a fee; of his last work he sold a mere hundred copies, with the result that no publisher can be found willing to try a new venture, even with the author covering the expense. How would anyone suspect that there is in this rather bland-looking character one of the most brilliant artistic minds the world has ever produced?

From his notebook (November 1887):

"Form, Style. An ideal monologue. All that has a learned appearance absorbed by the depths. All the accents of deep passion, anxiety and also weakness. Softenings, sun spots—brief happiness, sublime serenity.—Go beyond demonstrations; to be absolutely personal… Types of *Memories*; say the most abstract things in the most concrete and bloody way. The whole of history, as if it were lived and suffered personally (only then does it become true). —As much as possible, visible, precise things, examples… no description, all problems transposed in feeling, as far as passion."

Ah! That beguiling madman, our master! He was well over forty years too early, as he claimed. Don't we, too, want the whole of history to be lived and suffered personally? Already an author of "romanticized lives", this Nietzsche! Already an artist who transposes all problems into feeling. And who will lose the esteem of "serious" people. This philosopher is nothing but a poet. After *The Genealogy of Morals* was sent to Erwin Rohde, these two childhood friends never wrote another line to each other. Nietzsche returns to Nice. He resumes work relentlessly, with weariness but also a certain jubilance. Some nights, the distress and solitude become intolerable. "I have forty-three years behind me and I feel as lonely as if I were a child." All remains to be done and said. His work is still only the outline of an idea, a promise, and he would falter at his task if it were not for music. "She alone delivers me from myself, she sobers me up, orientates me towards myself, as if I looked down on myself from a great height, as if I had the sensation of being at a very high vantage point. She fortifies me, and regularly, following an evening of music (I have listened to *Carmen* now four times), a morning dawns redolent with energetic sights and discoveries. It is quite remarkable. It is as if I have bathed in a more neutral element. Life without music is simply a mistake, enfeeblement, an exile." (Letter to Gast.)

Thus the year 1888 commences. His boxes are enriched with hundreds of pages of notes towards the great final book. The intellectual engine is running at full throttle, but the clutch won't yet engage. He needs alternative roads, another sky. And it shall be Italy again. "My health, thanks to an extraordinarily beautiful winter, healthy food and long walks, has remained sufficiently robust. Nothing is sick save for the poor soul", he wrote on 31st March. Two days later he leaves for Turin.

The journey is burlesque: he catches the wrong train in Savona and enters a carriage bound for Genoa. He misplaces his luggage. He is obliged to see the city of Columbus again, this city "where one cannot be a coward", and his heart is overwhelmed with gratitude. Genoa is a fragment of his past before which he feels respect, so severe and lonely was his life there. "You don't take leave of this city without taking leave of yourself." Finally, crushed by fatigue, he reaches Turin. This capital revives him. Its streets in geometric lines, the Carignano Palace, the arcades, the formal gardens, all this exudes a joyful elegance, an ensemble of taste, the most delicate balance of the Latin seventeenth century. Royal avenues, aristocratic hotels, civilized people, all flatters his sense of hierarchies. The cafés radiate light, gold and marble. In the Turin directory he notes there are twelve theatres, an Accademia Filarmonica, a number of teachers of various instruments and the addresses of twenty-four composers. In short, a city of music. First-class bookshops. Excellent trattorias: meals for 1 fr. 25, ice cream and coffee at 0 fr. 20. As for the air, it comes straight down from the snow-capped Alps. Our blind man moves around with ease, straight-backed in his frayed garments. His fatigue has subsided. How light he feels here, to think and write! He is treated with deference: he is taken for a German officer. "From here we go to the king," he said. King of what? And go where? He always thought of departures, without suspecting that one day they would come to him. Now, the propeller will soon stop turning: we have reached the port.

X

Turinese Illuminations

W agner had three disciples. Three disciples only, but three
artists, three poets; and to all three had he not brought
ill fortune? Poor Richard! You could compose a ballad about it,
"The ballad of Richard, the disenchanted magician", or "The
ballad of Richard and the three madmen". Nietzsche chuckled
as he imagined at least one of these three would avenge the
other two.

First there was Baudelaire. To him, Wagner had written
in 1861 a spectacular letter thanking him for a famous article.
Having discovered it in a journal, Nietzsche copies it out in full
for Peter Gast. Here it is:

My dear Monsieur Baudelaire,

I was at your domicile on a number of occasions without
managing to find you. You will imagine how eager I am to
recount to you the immense satisfaction you have brought to
me by your article, which honours and encourages me to a
greater extent than anything that has been written about my
poor talent thus far. How would it not be possible to express

to you, aloud, how intoxicated I felt reading these sublime pages which communicated to me—as the best poem will—the impressions that I must boast of having produced upon a structure as superior as yours? I thank you a thousand times for this blessing you have bestowed on me, and understand that I am very proud to be able to call you a friend. See you soon, I very much hope?

Yours ever

Richard Wagner.

Nietzsche protested the style, the vanity. He went on: "A letter of this nature, with this air of familiarity and enthusiasm, I recall being written to someone else at quite another time: when Wagner received *The Birth of Tragedy*." Yes, Friedrich Nietzsche had been the recipient of one almost identical, ten years after Baudelaire. And Baudelaire had died half-insane, a paralytic. And when the "illustrious name" was pronounced before the stricken poet, he was said to have "smiled with joy".

Then there was King Ludwig II. One whose head was turned by the hurler of destiny, the great healer of music. Wagner both initiated and consummated his ruin. He drew him into madness, as Jupiter does those he wants to lose. And now he is dead. Drowned two years ago. Like Baudelaire, death from insanity, from solitude, from despair, from impossible grandeur. Perhaps death from poetry unexpressed.

And so to the last disciple, the third larcenist, the famous apostate. Ah! How he was going to fly to the rescue of his two colleagues, he, "the only German writer". Keep an eye out for his next pamphlets: *The Case of Wagner, Twilight of the Idols, The Antichrist*. Suddenly he would take vengeance on the two shadows that accompany him everywhere on his path, preventing him from getting too overheated, depriving him of sun; those he somewhere refers to as the great erotic chroniclers of the ideal: the Nazarene and the Bayreuthian.

Yet Nietzsche is upbeat. He "transvalues values", an arid affair; but the evenings are for leisure; the café terraces, *Carmen* (again and again), walks in these noble and splendid streets. And then more news arrives: Georg Brandes, in Copenhagen, gives a course on the philosophy of Nietzsche, and three hundred crowd in to hear him lecture. From New York, an admirer promises subsidies and a major critical essay. In addition, the philosopher's eyes and legs are not faring so badly here, in this more relaxing city. Sometimes Nietzsche even sings, composes burlesque verses. Yes, he is cheerful, "almost as much so as when attending a funeral".

Over the summer of that year he returns to Sils Maria, where he completes *The Case of Wagner*,[1] and writes *Twilight of the Idols* in a matter of weeks. These are books of vital importance for Nietzsche, where we witness not just furious outbursts but a kind of necessary conclusion to his ideas. Revenge on Wagner, for sure. But also a justification for this immense Nietzschean meditation which has lasted twenty years. He suffers from the fate of music as from an open wound. For this destiny has been distorted, its natural path thrown off course. Music is no longer a joy and an enlightenment, since Wagner, but a deep pain and a darkening. A music of decadence and a drowning-out of the pipes of Dionysus. These things have to be said over and again, so as to ensure that in future there will be no misunderstanding, as now, about the causes of the breakdown. He had to go over it all again, explain again, justify himself again. "In a flash I could have been utterly destroyed then, since I am not crude enough to know how to ruthlessly detach myself from the beings I have loved. Yet it was finally done, and still I live."

Andler rightly states that "the Nietzschean critique of European Romanticism, of which Wagner is such a powerful fragment, can only be judged in the light of his entire philosophy. Nietzsche is attached to this Romanticism by too many threads for him to be justified in condemning it wholesale, just as his roots also cling to the most Gallic classicism, so that he is perhaps the synthesis of classical art and Romantic art." But Nietzsche himself quite probably was not even aware. Over-exulted, febrile, sick, he embarks on his latest offensive to assert himself still more brilliantly. He labours whole nights, yet with a perfect lucidity of thought and an unprecedented cheerfulness of expression. At two o'clock in the morning, when his landlord Durisch departs for the Chamois hunt, Nietzsche is already bent over his writing table. "Who knows," he says, "maybe I, too, will chase some game over these summits." And he sinks the knife into old Richard, whose heroines, "as soon as you strip them of their heroic robes, resemble Madame Bovary".

In a few days he writes *The Antichrist*.[2] Make no mistake: this brilliant essay is not directed against the person of Jesus and his doctrine, but against his interpreters, the priests. Perhaps no single thinker or even poet felt and understood the person of Christ more sensitively than Nietzsche. For the partly apocryphal accounts which describe him are too doctored for us to be able to recognize in them the "Buddhist", or the tender face of the Galilean. Christ, as Nietzsche saw him, is a primitive poet of mankind who lacked a Dostoyevsky to show us how great purity of heart and the highest speculations of the mind are vitiated by popular simplicity and the distortions of their exploiters. It is they who made pain—and therefore sin—a necessity. And why? Because they made a living from it. They have made suffering their daily bread. How could they have led us to believe that true life, eternal life *is found*; not promised (provided we have paid our moral and material dues), but there, present, *within* us. The first disciples translated as best they could this being whom they could not properly grasp, a text awash with symbols and elusive things. Then all those who followed skewed it still further, according to their need or their pride. But Christ spoke only through concrete images. His kingdom is that of children; his faith is without rancour and without reprimand: it lives, it is itself its own miracle and reward. It has no need of prayers or theology, just practice. What Christ dethroned was the Judaism of the idea of sin, of forgiveness, all this dogmatism which was taken up and developed by the theologians of the West. Christ was teaching a new life, not a new faith. This is how he became love. Love never asks for a reward. And Nietzsche finds this expression admirable: "The kingdom of heaven is a state of the heart."

That's how our Antichrist sees it. Were we not right to say that he is in fact deeply Christian? Not Christian according to the Church, of course, but certainly in relation to Jesus. Frank Harris's[3] words on Oscar Wilde could equally well be applied to him: "To live like a disciple of Jesus was impossible for this Greek born out of season." And yet his work is in some places visibly evangelical. His life too. Both are bestowed from within. These are not theories, but a practice, and this great seer is closer to a Francis of Assisi. Only their two mouths could deliver a phrase like this: "The reign of God is not something that is expected, it has no yesterday and no day after tomorrow; it does not come in a thousand years; it is an experience of the heart: he is everywhere, he is nowhere." And then: "Do not defend yourself, do not become angry, do not blame… but also do not resist evil—*love evil*."

Here, Tolstoy emerges. But I have already shown what separates the muscular old peasant from this fragile aristocrat of the spirit. Sickness carves out an insurmountable intellectual abyss between these two living beings. In the anxious eye of the healthy one is always read the fear of death; the patient's delicate hand stretches out toward life, wants to grasp love, a love that sickness exalts because it alone provides ecstasy, the Dionysian summit of sensitivity. Intoxication, paralysis, ecstasy, epilepsy, insanity, all these are ranked together in the lofty mystery of the creative intelligence.

I am not afraid to repeat that Nietzsche loved and understood Christ better than all modern theologians. And this is still true even if one has to believe, as I once heard Gide say, that he was envious of Jesus. One can be envious out of admiration; and almost always out of love. By excess of love. Nietzsche's hatred is addressed only to Christians, because they have falsified the master's word. Because they did not understand why he died. Because they saw only the absurd idea of the atoning sacrifice instead of glorifying the example given, which is that of complete liberation of the spirit and its superiority over any idea of *ressentiment.*[4] The meaning of Christian death has for ever been estranged from it. And Saint Paul complicates this error even more, serving to annihilate this supreme lesson by considering only the risen Jesus. The saviour's *life* was of no use to him. All he needed was his *death*. The practice of Christianity as it emerges from its doctrine is by no means an ideal, but simply a recipe for finding happiness; a sort of cowardice in the face of true human greatness, which is unhappiness accepted, understood, overcome. And that's why Nietzsche wrote these terrible words about Christianity, these desperate words: "The Gospel died on the cross."

XI

Dionysus Crucified

Nietzsche returned to Turin towards the end of September and took up his room again with Davide Fino, a newsagent. It was located at the corner of Via Carlo Alberto, opposite the Carignano Palace. Mlle Fino put her piano at the disposal of the boarder, who liked to improvise on it at the end of the working day. Or he would visit Rosenberg and Sellier's bookstore to browse the newspapers and chat with the vendors. He avidly listens to music on the café terraces, he loves Audran's *La Mascotte*,[1] and flees when the orchestra takes on the *Zigeunerbaron*.[2] The air is delectable, calming. A warm and languid autumn; but deep in his body Nietzsche feels a genuine fear of winter. An "internal" cold. He hasn't felt too warm over recent months, so he treats himself to a thickly woven yet elegant garment from the best tailor. But he has never experienced such joie de vivre, felt so utterly at ease. Examining himself in his landlord's golden mirror, he observes a man ten years younger. Moreover, he knows he is appreciated in Turin, loved even. Waiters, for example, always reserve the best cuts for him. And what an appetite: he has never eaten so heartily.

To celebrate his birthday, he begins his intellectual biography *Ecce Homo*, or *How One Becomes What One Is*. The entire book is written between 15th October and 4th November, in the most agreeable of dispositions and before a landscape so soft-hued one might have been transported to the skies of Claude Lorrain. In town they are staging a beauty contest. The ladies pile their hair up as high as possible, suck in their waists and push out their posteriors under "bustles". Nietzsche's lightness of mind is such that he only has taste for the operetta, a Parisian genre of the highest taste, the most exquisite refinement. This moment of his dying life reminds one of the Stendhalian beginning of the author's letters on Metastasio: "The common man easily despises grace. It is characteristic of common souls to esteem only what they are a little in fear of." Doesn't Nietzsche remember being the first to say, "All that is good is light; all that is divine runs on delicate feet"? We ought to turn *The Case of Wagner* into an operetta, he suggests to Gast. And he confesses that, though he is writing in German, in truth he thinks only of his French readers.

Such, the moment he relaxes for an instant, is the Nietzsche of his latest book, the newest, the most powerful of all: *The Will to Power*.[3] We, who know the tragedy which is brewing, are watching on this poor face for the first signs of downfall. Nothing as yet. Never has this indefatigable labourer found himself so lucidly at ease in terms of irony and disdain; that hand so sure to cut cleanly through flesh decomposed by morality. With the surgeon's skill he performs, he cuts, he ligatures, in pursuit of the only truth: life. But psychiatrists have recognized, it is said, that episodes of madness are often preceded by these expansive, fruitful, calm periods where the intelligence is suddenly magnified. Nietzsche works frantically, as if he had already been warned that tomorrow no longer belongs to him.

One Sunday at the end of November he attends a concert, where he experiences one of the most forceful impressions of his life. But he notes that he is incapable of suppressing a perpetual grimace from breaking out on his face. On the pro-gramme: the *Egmont* overture by Beethoven, the "Hungarian March" by Liszt, then a piece by the Italian Rossaro ("I haven't a clue what the big names mean any more... perhaps the best remains unknown"); the opening of *Sakuntala* by Goldmark, the air "Cypris" by Renaud de Vilbac, and finally "Patrie", by Bizet.[4] To master his abundant pleasure, Nietzsche manages only the grimace of tears. Broken, yet serene, assured, beatific, such is this foreign listener, unknown to the crowd, he who has just completed five works in a matter of weeks.

Ecce Homo has gone to his publisher. It is dynamite and is going to blow history in two. Strindberg writes to him. A Russian princess too; Georg Brandes announces he is set to give a new course on his philosophy. Nietzsche takes the opportunity to reread his own works. He feels electrified: it seems that only now is he beginning to understand it, to grasp its scope. And suddenly, on 6th December, with *Ecce Homo,* the publication of which he has decided to delay, comes this strange forebod-ing: "I do not see why I should hasten too much the tragic catastrophe of my life, which begins with *Ecce.*" Ought we to take note of this too, in a postscript to Peter Gast: "All those who have anything to do with me now, even the fruit seller who selects beautiful grapes for me, are perfectly accomplished beings, most wise, joyous, somewhat overweight, down to the café waiters!"? Are these signs of encroaching insanity? Let's be clear, here and now, that we don't think so. Not even the childish joy he has at a brief letter from Taine, which makes him cry out: "The Grand Canal from Panama to France is now open to me" seems suspicious.

Christmas. From his little room in Via Carlo Alberto, Nietzsche listens to the latest music from the café opposite (*The Barber of Seville*), the last music his mind will know. The shadow is suddenly filled with the voices of his beloved and despised heroes: Jesus, Caesar, Wagner, Dionysus, Zarathustra. It overcomes his brain. A shadow full of soft light, mysterious reconciliations, tender dreams, personified grandeur. The symbolic faces that for so many years provided images to accompany his thought suddenly rise from their intellectual night and dazzle the remaining sight of the wretched blind man. He laughs. He hails them. He accepts them in turn.

What a Christmas, this year of 1888! Omnipotence, love, pity, kindness, harshness, all that he loved and all that he condemned invade his shattered soul. When you wear ten crowns, possess twenty hearts, the sum of the wisdom and foolishness of men, how should you properly remember the humble name your father bequeathed you? However, neither his landlord, nor the waiters who serve him, nor the patrons of the café he frequents, no one suspects that this solitary and reserved stranger has over the course of the last few hours gone insane. He takes up his pen and begins to write. Finally, the world, the vast world where so many deaf and blind shades circulate, will now receive news from the only living great one, who has forgotten his own name.

On 28th December he writes to Professor Overbeck, his former colleague from Basel, that he is intending to unite all

European courts in an anti-German league and bind his homeland in an iron shirt.

On the 31st he sends these lines to Gast:

"Friend, what a moment!... It was the famous Rubicon. I don't know my address. Let's just say it is: the Quirinal Palace."

Then to Strindberg, who had just sent him one of his stories:

Dear Sir

You will have a response to your news shortly. It will arrive like a gunshot. I gave the order to convene a Congress of Sovereign heads in Rome and I am of a mind to have the young emperor shot. Goodbye! For we will meet again, but on one condition, let's get divorced.

Nietzsche Caesar

On one of those tragic days, as he was out on a walk, something happened when he saw a bully of a carter striking his horse about the head. Should he have simply passed on, the man who had made pity the mother of all spiritual vices? Nietzsche apparently launched himself around the animal's neck and fervently embraced it. A moment later he was helped away, stricken with apoplexy, and his landlord Davide Fino was on hand to escort him home. Nietzsche remained in a lethargic slumber for two days, then abruptly his body awakened, but the brain remained dormant for ever. Right away, he took up his old correspondence...

To Burckhardt in Basel:

"I am Ferdinand de Lesseps... I have been entombed twice this autumn... I salute the immortal M. Daudet, for he is one of the forty."

To Peter Gast

"Sing me a new song; the world is transfigured and the heavens rejoice.

The Crucified."

Finally, to Cosima Wagner, this unhinged tiny note, distant awakening of an ancient pain:

"Ariadne, I love you.

Dionysus."

As the funeral of Prince Admiral Eugène de Savoie-Carignan was unfolding with great pomp, Nietzsche watched the officers, dignitaries, diplomats and the whole court parade beneath his windows. He had the notion he was attending his own state funeral, then rushed down to join the crowd, claiming he was Cardinal Antonelli.[5] Running on towards the station, he accosted passers-by: "Be joyful," he said to them, "I am God. I am just in disguise."

Everything he abhorred and which lay submerged deep within rises now to his mouth like vomit. A pitiful wreck, he returns home and remains confined there, on occasion performing satyr-like dances, or assailing Mlle Fino's piano, the keys of which he crushes in the most horrible dissonance. Finally, on 9th January of the new year (1889), Overbeck opens the door and Nietzsche falls gratefully into his arms, addresses him in Italian and breaks into sobbing.

The faithful friend then took the madman away without the latter offering the least resistance. During the journey that removed him from Italian soil for ever, they barely exchanged a handful of words. Only once did Nietzsche suddenly break out in song. It was the song of the Venetian gondolier, which the poet had just inserted into *Ecce Homo*,

and Overbeck was struck by the admirable melody sustained
by the insane man:

> Leaning on the bridge
> I stood in the brown night.
> From the distance a song welled up to me.
> Drops of gold were streaming
> On the quivering face of the water.
> Gondolas, lights, music.
> It was all drifting towards dusk.
> My soul the chord of a harp
> Sang to itself,
> Invisibly touched,
> A gondolier's song,
> Trembling with multi-coloured bliss.
> Is anyone listening to him?

Friedrich Nietzsche lived on for more than ten years. He never
recovered his sanity. The recognition and celebrity once denied
him now overwhelmed the oblivious genius. European youth
finally recognized as one of their key masters this invalid pros-
trate on a chaise longue, now dead to all intelligence and permanently struck down by a god as ruthless as himself. His mother
and sister first moved to the clinic where he was being treated
in Jena. Then the healthy sales of Nietzsche's books (so long
awaited in vain) made it possible to raise the sums needed to
care for the poor incurable, who had his whole life long only
known shabby "furnished" rooms, in a handsome house in
Weimar, where Goethe, Schiller, Herder and Liszt had paraded
their glory. It was decorated with some taste, and his books

and papers surrounded him there. Month by month and year by year, they patiently waited and watched to see when this spectre might awaken. But that hour never came. On occasion, though, a glimmer of the past seemed to light up his features.

"Haven't I written some fine books?" he once asked.

On another occasion, seeing his sister's face stained with tears, he said:

"Lisbeth, but why on earth are you crying? Are we not happy?"

And when he was shown Wagner's portrait:

"That one, yes I liked him very much."

Does all this not recall a bedridden Baudelaire "smiling with joy" before the same face at the time when his intelligence, too, had withered? Ten years of purely vegetative life. Yet he had become handsome, the philosopher, his face more refined, the hands impressive despite their thinness. He was clothed in an all-white fleece tunic, like a priest's stole. Friends were allowed to pay visits. One of the last he received, in August 1900, was that of ex-Mlle von der Pahlen, who had become Baroness von Ungern-Sternberg, the lady with whom Nietzsche shared a journey on his first trip to Italy, twenty-four years earlier. Did he recognize her? We cannot know. He fixed his wide, gentle gaze on her, the gaze that seemed to see much further now that he was not wearing spectacles, and he smiled. Peter Gast, who also visited, played music, and Nietzsche would clap his pale hands together for a long time. Perhaps amongst the last things he understood was the profound speech of this piano, of this friend, whose inner music he had always been—and still was—the only one to hear. But no thought, no word emerged from this ruinate soul. Nietzsche expired, walled up in his silence. Thus was extinguished a pure heart, which no one, his sister and a friend excepted, had ever known how to love.

I witnessed this room, this bed, and the final portrait of the invalid, with his wildly open, fixed eye searching to remember. "Now," he seemed to say, "I command you to lose me and find yourselves."

PARIS, JULY 1929

Notes

I. A TRAVELLER WITHOUT BAGGAGE

1 Refers to Chemins de fer de Paris à Lyon et à la Méditerranée.
2 *The Birth of Tragedy: Out of the Spirit of Music* was Nietzsche's first book, published in 1872, and concerns the opposing forces of the Dionysian and Apollonian and their fusing, which resulted in the development of poetry and in particular Greek tragedy. The final part of the book is a lyrical clarion call to the reader to experience spiritual rebirth through Wagner's music.
3 *Untimely Meditations* consists of four essays by Nietzsche published between 1873 and 1876, which are profoundly influenced by the thought of Schopenhauer and the music of Wagner.
4 *Richard Wagner in Bayreuth* is the fourth essay in the *Untimely Meditations*, first published in 1876.

II. PORT-ROYAL OF SORRENTO

1 Pourtalès appears to be referring here to the religious community from the abbey of Port-Royal des Champs, situated about nine miles from Versailles, which in 1626 relocated to the rue Faubourg Saint-Jacques in Paris and became a stronghold of Jansenism.

2 *Memories of an Idealist* was first published in French in Switzerland, then, seven years later, in 1876, the German-language version *Memoiren einer Idealistin* appeared with Schuster and Loeffler in Stuttgart.

3 Referring to the wave of revolutions against the prevailing conservative social order which swept Europe in 1848.

4 *Human, All Too Human: A Book for Free Spirits* was first published in 1878. Here in his so-called "middle period" Nietzsche ushers in the aphoristic style taken from La Rochefoucauld which would mark his later writings and decisively breaks with Romanticism, following the severance with Wagner in 1876.

III. VENETIAN MUSIC

1 *Tristan and Isolde* is the celebrated opera in three acts by Wagner which premiered in Munich in 1865.

2 *Dawn* or *Daybreak* appeared in 1881 and the five books of which it is composed are dominated by the aphoristic style for which Nietzsche would be renowned. This is the first stage of Nietzsche's mature period and his "revaluation of all values", which will reach its zenith with *Zarathustra* and *The Genealogy of Morals*.

3 The neoclassical Palazzo Berlendis is situated at the end of the Rio dei Mendicanti Canal in Venice and looks out towards the cemetery island of Isola di San Michele. This quiet location apart from the touristic enclaves was Nietzsche's favoured residence in the city from 1880 to 1887.

4 Pylades and Orestes were figures from Homeric legend who enjoyed a peculiarly strong bond of friendship and have since become bywords for faith and love in Greek culture.

5 Princess Carolyne zu Sayn-Wittgenstein (1819–87) was a Polish aristocrat who experienced a forty-year relationship with Liszt, and an amateur journalist and essayist who is thought to have been the author of much of the text in his landmark *Life of Chopin* published in 1852.

6 Goethe's *Journey to Italy* or *Italian Journey* is a report on his travels in Italy between 1786 and 1788, which began as a series of letters made during the journey. It was transformed into a journal filled with valuable observations on art and history, nature and the character of the local people in Rome, Naples, Sicily and Venice.

7 *Manfred* is a dramatic poem by Lord Byron dating from 1816–17. The poem, known as a closet drama, deals with themes of guilt and is couched in the supernatural, suggesting a taste for English ghost stories of the time.

8 *Ecce Homo: How One Becomes What One Is* was written in 1888 but not published until after Nietzsche's death in 1908. It represents Nietzsche's own interpretation of his works and their future significance. It constitutes the last original text he wrote before his final period of mental confusion.

9 *The Siegfried Idyll* is a symphonic poem for chamber orchestra which Wagner composed as a birthday gift for his second wife Cosima, after the birth of their son Siegfried in 1869. Wagner's opera *Siegfried*, premiered in 1876, draws on music from the *Idyll*.

10The Palazzo Giustiniani in Rome, also known as Piccolo Colle or "Little Hill", was built near the Pantheon at the end of the sixteenth century. It long served as a repository of art, lined with paintings by Titian, Caravaggio and Raphael.

IV. PICCOLO SANTO GENOVESE

1 Charles Philippe Théodore Andler (1866–1933) was a French Germanist and philosopher whose writings included important texts on socialism and communism. His *Nietzsche, sa vie et sa pensée* (*Nietzsche, His Life and Thought*) was published in six volumes in 1920.

2 *Rhumbs*, Paul Valéry.

3 Pforta refers to a school housed in the Pforta monastery, near Naumburg in Saxony-Anhalt. The name originates from Pforta Coeli

(Gate of Heaven). Nietzsche entered the highly respected boarding school in 1858 after winning a scholarship. To be a boarder at the exclusive Pforta had apparently been Nietzsche's childhood dream. He remained a pupil there until 1864.

V. ZARATHUSTRA—LOVER OF CARMEN

1 "Hymnus an das Leben" ("Hymn to Life") is a musical composition for chorus and orchestra which was published in Leipzig in the summer of 1887. Nietzsche's musical creations have traditionally been seen as interesting but insubstantial curiosities beside the greatness of his philosophical writings, yet, as Pourtalès is keen to demonstrate, Nietzsche himself saw his musical creations as a vital accompaniment to his thought, and in *Nietzsche in Italy* is at pains to promote this link. For example, in October 1887, Nietzsche wrote a letter to the German conductor Felix Mottl: "I wish that this piece of music may stand as a complement to the word of the philosopher which, in the manner of words, must remain by necessity unclear. The affect of my philosophy finds its expression in this hymn."

2 Doria is the name of a wealthy aristocratic Genoese family of long lineage who played a central role in the history of the Republic of Genoa from the twelfth to the sixteenth centuries.

3 *The Gay Science*, or, as it was first known, *The Joyful Wisdom*, was first published in 1882. A second edition followed in 1887, after the completion of *Thus Spoke Zarathustra* and *Beyond Good and Evil*. The expanded edition includes an appendix of songs. The title derives from the Provençal expression *"gai saber"*, the technique or "science" of writing poetry, exemplified by the period of the troubadours. Nietzsche saw the knightly poets as the admirable rootstock of the "Good European" free spirits he was extolling: passionate, inventive, heroic and life-affirming.

4 The romantic gardens of the Villetta Negro and its Tombe di Negro,

built in 1861, have long been a place of pilgrimage, a must-stop for foreign writer travellers, most notably before Nietzsche: George Sand, Madame de Staël, Lord Byron, Charles Dickens, Honoré de Balzac and Stendhal.

5 *Idylls from Messina* comprises a set of eight poems written by Nietzsche in Sicily during the spring of 1882. Six of them ended up in slightly modified form in the second edition of *The Gay Science* in 1887.

VI. MLLE LOU ON NAXOS

1 Although she was Russian-born, to Protestant parents of French Huguenot and German descent, Salomé was dubbed a "Finnish Jew" by the Nazis, a falsity which, as evidenced here, clearly preceded their denunciation of her.

2 Pourtalès is here presumably referring to the now-infamous staged studio image dating from 1882 of Nietzsche and Rée "harnessed" by reins to a miniature cart (not a wheelbarrow), on which Lou Salomé kneels, holding the other end of the reins in one hand and an absurd toy whip in the other. According to Salomé in her memoirs, it was a playful Nietzsche who organized this folly, though Rée, who had a loathing for any pictorial reproductions of himself, was hardly a willing participant. There is a notable stiffness and awkwardness in the poses, save for Nietzsche, who summons an uncanny visionary gaze. Pourtalès implies this staged scene occurred in Orta, but it was more likely to have been shortly after, in Lucerne.

3 Nietzsche referred to Cosima Wagner as Ariadne, the daughter of King Minos of Crete and immortal wife of Dionysus. In *Ecce Homo* he asks cryptically: "Who, besides me, knows what Ariadne is?", but the name appears most famously in a sequence of his last letters, after his mental collapse in Turin on 3rd January 1889, where he addresses "Princess Ariadne" and concludes with the brief desperate note, "Ariadne, I love you, Dionysus."

4 André Gide's *Les Nourritures terrestres* (*Fruits of the Earth*) was first published in 1897.

5 Charles du Bos (1882–1939) was an essayist and critic of French and English literature, whose illustrious subjects included Goethe, Shakespeare, Shelley, Keats and Byron. He was influenced by the thought of Georg Simmel, Henri Bergson and Nietzsche. His *Dialogue avec André Gide* was published in Paris in 1929, the same year as *Nietzsche in Italy*.

6 *Thus Spoke Zarathustra: A Book for All And for No One* was written and published between 1883 and 1885. It is Nietzsche's globally most renowned work, and, though sometimes classed as a "philosophical novel", it is essentially a series of dazzling aphorisms, a visionary amalgam of prose and poetry delivered from the lips of the sage Zarathustra (based on the Persian prophet Zoroaster).

VII. DEAD GODS AND THE LIVING PROPHET

1 Nietzsche's "Night Song" is incorporated into Part 2 of his *Zarathustra*: "But I live in my very own light, I drink back the flames that leap up within me…"

2 Georg Brandes (1842–1927) was an influential Danish music critic and scholar who was instrumental in bringing Scandinavian culture to the attention of the rest of Europe from the 1870s onwards. His mission was to liberate Denmark from its provincial isolation, through championing writers such as August Strindberg and Jens Peter Jacobsen. He was profoundly influenced by Nietzsche's writings in the late 1880s, leading him to develop his own philosophy of aristocratic radicalism.

3 Pourtalès refers to the villa known as "Château Balsan", built by Colonel Jacques Balsan for his wife Consuelo Vanderbilt, who was divorced from the 9th Duke of Marlborough. "Lou Seuil", as the villa was first called, is conceived like a monastery, complete with cloister, bell tower and chapel. It was inspired by the Convent of Le Thoronet in the Var region of Provence.

VIII. HE LEAVES A COUNTRY INHABITED BY NO ONE

1 Ferdinando Galiani (1728–87) was an Italian economist and leading figure of the Enlightenment who Nietzsche believed possessed "a most fastidious and refined intelligence". Galiani's letters are considered of importance, for they provide a valuable insight into the economic, social and political life of eighteenth-century Europe. His correspondents included Voltaire and Diderot.

2 Domenico Cimarosa (1749–1801) was an Italian composer of the Neapolitan school who wrote a large number of comic operas, as well as choral works and instrumental music.

3 Niccolò Piccinni (1728–1800) was an Italian composer best known for his operas and as a rival of the better-remembered Gluck.

4 The Cimitero delle Porte Sante of San Miniato al Monte was opened in 1847 and is the chosen sanctuary for illustrious Florentines. It is one of the great monumental cemeteries of Italy, boasting an impressive range of monuments and funerary sculpture. As Pourtalès attests, the cemetery also offers a majestic view over Florence and offers a haven of peace a world away from the crowded city below.

5 *Beyond Good and Evil: Prelude to a Philosophy of the Future* was published in 1886 and expands on the thought expressed in *Zarathustra*, but resorts to the earlier aphoristic style. Famous Nietzschean preoccupations such as "the will to power", "master and slave morality" and "the free spirit" are fully expressed here, amidst vigorous assaults on stoicism, dogmatism, physics and German nationalism.

6 Charles Maurras (1868–1952) was a French author and politician who gave birth to the counter-revolutionary doctrine of *Maurrassisme*, which favoured classicism over Romanticism and the domination of reason in philosophy, and monarchism, with the Catholic Church as

guarantor of order and stability. *Maurrassisme* was finally discredited, after its links with the odious Pétain regime in Vichy France during the Second World War.

IX. ALL PROBLEMS TRANSPOSED IN FEELING

1 *Ecce Homo.*

2 *On the Genealogy of Morals: A Polemic* was published in 1887 and returns to themes found in *Beyond Good and Evil*. It is considered by some to be Nietzsche's most impressive work.

X. TURINESE ILLUMINATIONS

1 *The Case of Wagner: A Musician's Problem* was published in 1888. It is Nietzsche's determined critique of Wagner and his music, the antipode to his effusive praise found in earlier works such as *The Birth of Tragedy* and *Untimely Meditations.* Nietzsche's disillusion with Wagner and the necessity he felt to extricate himself from the composer's spell is first made clear in *Human, All Too Human* of 1878.

2 *The Anti-Christ*, or as it could otherwise be translated, *The Anti-Christian*, was written in 1888, but its publication was, like that of *Ecce Homo*, delayed by Overbeck and Köselitz due to its provocative content. Here, Nietzsche tenaciously espouses a philosophy finally liberated from false gods such as Wagner, the inveigling priestly theology which he felt had compromised Kant, the life-denying pessimism of Schopenhauer, etc. Priests come in for the most scathing denunciation, most memorably as "attorneys of mere emptiness".

3 Frank Harris (1856–1931) was an Irish-American novelist, journalist and publisher who relocated to England, where he edited literary journals such as *The Saturday Review*. He wrote biographies of Oscar Wilde and George Bernard Shaw, but was best known for his racy autobiography *My Life and Loves*, in four volumes (1923–27).

4 *Ressentiment*, one of the key Nietzschean ideas, denotes the reaction to suffering where the individual experiencing pain finds a scapegoat in another to ease their affliction. A desire for revenge against one's own inferiority or failure is turned against an external strength, thus in Nietzsche's view the weak attack the strong, noble, heroic strain and cling to illusions of equality to uphold their lowliness. Negative valuations are not born of a truth but rather out of a need to escape an unwanted condition or position.

XI. DIONYSUS CRUCIFIED

1 *La Mascotte* is a three-act comic operetta dating from 1880, with music by Edmond Audran (1840–1901).

2 *Der Zigeunerbaron* (*The Gypsy Baron*) is an operetta, or arguably a comic opera, in three acts by Johann Strauss II (1825–99), which was only outstripped in popularity during Strauss's lifetime by *Die Fledermaus*.

3 *The Will to Power* was compiled from Nietzsche's notebooks from 1883 to 1888, and published by his sister Elisabeth Förster-Nietzsche in 1901. But Nietzsche was working on a book with this title on the eve of his descent into madness, and the posthumous publication of the compilation of notes employs that title. Subjects include the whole Nietzschean panorama of art, religion, morality, the theory of knowledge and any other topic which drew the philosopher's gaze. Elisabeth Förster-Nietzsche's notorious meddling with her brother's manuscripts, including the forging of letters and rewriting, constituted a flagrant misinterpretation of his thought to accord with her own prejudice. Her toxic editorial presence and courting of Hitler was largely responsible for Nietzsche's philosophy being viewed as a cornerstone of Nazi ideology.

4 Carlo Rossaro (1827–78) was a famed Italian pianist and composer of chamber music, who was also a fanatical devotee of Wagner and dedicated a piano sonata to the composer.

Karl Goldmark (1830–1915 was a Hungarian-born Viennese composer and another committed Wagnerian whose opera *Die Königin von Saba* (*The Queen of Sheba*) was very popular at the end of the nineteenth century. Renaud de Vilbac (1829–1884) was a prolific French organist and composer who wrote music for piano, organ and harmonium during the 1870s and 1880s and won the coveted Prix de Rome for one of his cantatas.

5 Giacomo Antonelli (1806–76), often known as the "Italian Richelieu", was cardinal and secretary to the Pope Pius IX and played an instrumental role in Italian politics.

Nietzsche Chronology

1844   Born on 15th October at Röcken, Prussian Saxony.

1849   Death of his father, a Lutheran pastor, on 30th July.

1850   The family Nietzsche moves to Naumburg.

1858–64   Attends boarding school at Schulpforta.

1864   Studies classical philology at Bonn University.

1865   Continues studies at Leipzig and discovers Schopenhauer's key works in a second-hand bookstore.

1868   First meeting with Richard Wagner.

1869   Becomes Professor of Classical Philology at the University of Basel.

1870   Volunteers as a medical orderly in the Franco–Prussian War and serves briefly with Prussian forces. Returns to Basel in October, physically broken.

1872   Publication of his first book, *The Birth of Tragedy*.

1872–73   Lectures on "The History of Greek Eloquence" to an almost empty room.

1873   Publication of the first of his *Untimely Meditations*. Also writes "Philosophy in the Tragic Age of the Greeks", based upon texts for a course of lectures on Pre-Platonic philosophy. Writes "On the Truth and Lies in a Nonmoral Sense", which is never completed.

1873–74   Prepares notes for a course of lectures on classical rhetoric in the summer semester, but a lack of interest causes it to be shelved.

1874   "Schopenhauer as Educator" is published as the third *Untimely Meditation*.

1876   "Richard Wagner in Bayreuth" is finally published, the last of the *Untimely Meditations*. Continues to lecture on Pre-Platonic philosophy, but his health severely declines. Leaves the university and travels to Sorrento.

1878   *Human, All Too Human* is published.

1879   Official resignation from university post. *Mixed Opinions and Maxims* published as an appendix to *Human, All Too Human*. Spends the summer in the Engadin.

1880   *The Wanderer and His Shadow* appears as a final addendum to *Human, All Too Human*.

1881   *Dawn* published. Spends the winter and spring in Genoa, summer in Sils Maria in Engadin. Returns to Genoa in the autumn.

1882   Publication of *The Gay Science*. Spends the winter in Genoa, spring in Messina, summer in Tautenburg with Lou Salomé and his sister Elisabeth. To Leipzig in the autumn, and then Rapallo in November.

1883   Writes Part I of *Thus Spoke Zarathustra* in Rapallo over the winter; spends early spring in Genoa, May in Rome, and in the summer returns to Sils Maria, where Part II is completed. Both parts are published separately in 1883. Nietzsche will now spend every summer in Sils Maria until 1888.

1884   Writes Part III of *Zarathustra* in Nice, in January.

1885   Part IV of *Zarathustra* written during the winter in Nice and Mentone. Forty copies are privately printed, but only a handful find readers amongst his remaining friends.

1886   Publication of *Beyond Good and Evil*. Adds a new preface to the remaining copies of both previous editions of *The Birth of Tragedy* (1872 and 1878). Second edition of *Human, All Too Human* appears.

1887   *On the Genealogy of Morals* is published. A second edition of *Dawn* appears with a new preface, and also of *The Gay Science*, with a newly added fifth book and an appendix of poems.

1888   Winter is spent in Nice, spring in Turin, summer in Sils Maria and autumn in Turin. *The Case of Wagner* appears. Georg Brandes gives lectures on Nietzsche's thought at the University of Copenhagen. Nietzsche's name begins to spread.

1889   Nietzsche becomes insane in early January in Turin. The loyal Overbeck escorts the stricken philosopher back to Basel. He enters the asylum in Jena, but is soon released into the care of his mother, who takes him to Naumburg. *Twilight of the Idols*, written in 1888, appears in January.

1895   *The Anti-Christ* and *Nietzsche contra Wagner*, both written in 1888, are finally published in volume eight of Nietzsche's collected works.

1897   Nietzsche's mother dies. His sister Elisabeth takes full control and moves him to Weimar.

1900   Dies on 25th August in the Villa Silberblick in Weimar.

1901   Elisabeth publishes some 400 of his notes, many of which he had already made use of, in volume fifteen of the collected works, under the title *The Will to Power*. It is later found that his self-appointed guardian and executor amended, fabricated and falsified Nietzsche's writings to suit her own racial prejudices, personal antipathies and political preference.

1904   Elisabeth integrates 200 pages of further material from *The Will to Power* into the last volume of her biography, *The Life of Friedrich Nietzsche*.

1908   First publication of *Ecce Homo*, originally written in 1888.